A MAN
With
THE WHITE COAT

LOM HARSH

Clever Fox
PUBLISHING

Chennai • Bangalore

CLEVER FOX PUBLISHING
Chennai, India

Published by CLEVER FOX PUBLISHING 2022
Copyright © LOM HARSH 2022

Disclaimer

The book is based on the life journey of Dr. Sunil Kumar Garssa as well as many other doctors like him. After conducting extensive research, interviewing, and consulting with major medical practitioners and doctors, this book was developed.

Despite the fact that some of the incidents in this book are inspired by true events, some of the scenarios and scenes are designed for readers in a fictional way.

DEDICATION

I dedicate this book to all the living gods in this world and beyond, who always stand and fight with their weapon of Hard work, Unsown Love and Sacrifices for the people striving for their good health.

CONTENTS

INTRODUCTION

The dying fire was meekly glowing at the steps of the porch of the ground guard's little hut. Heaps of dried, half-burnt leaves lay strewn around the fire; most were entirely charred. The dense pungent smoke from the diminishing flames choked the old man, disrupting his deep slumber. He coughed back to wakefulness and wiped the saliva from the sides of his mouth that resulted from the way he had slept all night, with his head hanging to one side. Putting on his glasses, he looked around. The day had not broken yet and it was cold, dark and still. Heavy fog had enveloped the entire premises in a smoky cloak. He looked up at the sky. It looked dark, blue-grey. Dawn was a few minutes away. He did not arise from the chair where he had dozed off last night and lazily waited for the distant little clinking sound of keys banging against the massive iron gates. It was his daily morning alarm.

It was a regular daybreak at the hospital ground premises. The old guard kept an ear out attentively and waited. The gates were far from where his quarters were, yet the silence of an early winter-morning of Jaipur always made it effortless for the faintest of noises to reach his ears. And he finally heard the clanging. The garden sweeper had arrived. The guard arose. He was the only one he welcomed every morning with a broad smile, especially during the winters. And why wouldn't he? After all he had obliged his request of piling up the dry leaves and carrying them to the old guard's porch every morning for a little warmth each night.

The old man started walking towards the gate searching for the keys in his pockets and at the same time cursing in a whisper, "Why does he have to come so early every morning? Just an hour ago another moron had turned up at the gates. Nobody will let me get a proper night's sleep tonight."

The gate was still a yard ahead of him. The haze of the fog and low light made it difficult for him to see anything beyond the gate except the very well-known traffic-light red winter cap peeping in between the grills which assured him it was the garden-sweeper. It was obvious though, since who else could bang the gates at this hour of a chilly, winter dawn?"Good morning, old man!" said the man standing outside the gates as the old guard put his keys into the keyhole.

He yawned in response. Then remembering his generosities, he smiled animatedly, "Come in," holding the gates narrowly open for him.

No sooner had he opened the gates than few people suddenly barged in from nowhere. They briskly pushed the sweeper aside and forcefully dragged the gates wide open from both sides making an annoying, grazing sound of metal scraping heavily against gravels.

"Wait! Stop! What are you doing?" shouted the startled old man.

The men ignored him like he didn't exist. As he kept on shouting, more and more men and women stormed in through the gates. The old guard gradually stopped yelling and stood there petrified, watching the mob carrying rods, sticks and stones rush inside the premises.

⚜

"Sir, BP is high," alerted the young doctor monitoring the blood pressure of the patient.

"Push a Beta blocker," commanded the senior cardiologist as he watched the bleeding spurt in the nineteen-year-old boy's artery with each successive heartbeat. Increasing volumes of blood than the previous one through the vessels had fallen prey to his operating tools.

"Sir, I pushed it right before the procedure started and his systolic was 140 and diastolic 90."

"What were the measures before you pushed Beta blocker?"

"Sir, 170 and 110mm-Hg"

"And how could you release him for the Cathlab!"

The young man looked at the senior doctor startled. He commanded again without raising his eyes from his patient as his bloodied hands worked tirelessly to close the puncture site,

"Push a beta blocker immediately."

"Sir, I had ordered one and I already pushed 2.5mg. I am ordering another, Sir..." said the doctor, lowering his eyes and quickly wrote down a beta blocker and held it out to a nurse. The nurse took it and opened the door to go out.

"Sunita, wait. Sharma, go with her," commanded the Matron.

As they closed the Cathlab door behind them and ran towards the medicine hall, Sunita expressed her regret, "How could a doctor overlook such a case? Working with Sir, even we have come to learn that perioperative and elective cases must be canceled if the systolic is 160 or above and diastolic 100 and above..."

"You are a little mistaken. It is not that such elective cases must be canceled. It is advisable that it should be canceled for avoiding risks of complication during procedure. But we have grown up here learning that it must be canceled since our Sir would never allow taking chance on patients' lives if the situation is avoidable."

"Nowadays we should be extra cautious at medical practice. It does not matter how many lives you save but if something happens to a very, high-risk patient, no one spares you."

"Are you listening?" asked Sunita.

Sharma heard faint garbled noises of commotion coming from downstairs, "Did you hear something? Something like people shouting?"

"No…" she listened attentively for a few seconds, "No, I don't hear anything."

They were not even two floors downstairs that both of them clearly heard shouts of outrage and wild banging on the hospital gate. As they were crossing the lobby at the end of which lay the ways to the main entrance and the Medicine Hall, they were stopped by some panicked hospital staffs.

"Don't go any further, Mam, a wild angry mob is wreaking havoc. We have somehow held them outside the gates, but the way they are constantly banging on it, throwing things at any hospital staff that come in front of them, doesn't make it safe any longer, it can collapse any moment. Please leave the hospital building through the back gate."

They could hear loud bangs and angry yells calling their chief Cardiologist names and bad words as though the people were throwing up a lifetime of hatred. They could see their path ahead that crossed the way to the main entrance littered with they didn't know what. Stones, bricks, metals, sharp objects, even water filled glass bottles; they left not a thing to injure the hospital staffs. Whenever any staff was crossing that pathway, they were being attacked with those objects. Sunita and Sharma looked at each other. They had been entrusted by the veteran Cardiologist Dr. Sunil, with the responsibility of saving a patient's life. They couldn't step back now and let him down. They started running again towards the Medicine Hall that lay at the end of the corridor. But to reach there they would have to cross the way to the entrance on their left. And without a doubt they would be attacked. They quickly ran across, deftly balancing, careful not to trip over the heap of litter on the floor. Many heavy objects and stones flew in their direction targeting them but all missed the hit.

They quickly entered the Medicine Hall and were shocked to find few of the glass windows broken to pieces in here too. Pieces of broken glass bottles and windowpanes lay strewn inside here and there. Life-saving drugs and medicines lay wasted, on the floors and over the racks. They stumbled upon few rolling broken bottles. Few times they skidded on the floor wetted by medicinal liquids and chemicals. They hurriedly started to search the racks and shelves; it was becoming difficult to maintain their sanity and find out the thing they had come looking for in a multitude of drugs.

Suddenly a heavy paper weight flew in through the broken window glass and shattered two bottles of drugs kept on the rack Sunita was browsing through, and toppled another, emptying its contents on the floor. The intrusion alert alarms had gone off blaring loudly and they felt like intruders themselves as they browsed through the racks. They prayed intently to get out of there as soon as possible with an intact dose of Beta Blocker; a drug used both during surgery and preoperatively to lower the blood pressure and heart rate of a patient since there are high chances that a patient undergoing surgery could experience a spike in BP during the surgery session which could result in fatality and death. Every second of delay would push the young boy a step towards death. They were finally relieved to find one bottle and rushed out with it into the lobby again.

As they crossed the entrance way again, a broken glass bottle hit Sunita in the right cheek leaving a deep gash. But they did not stop. They ran out of the mayhem and reached the Cathlab and held the drug over to the doctor who was in charge of maintaining the patient's BP.

Everyone looked at her bleeding wound waiting for an answer to an unasked question. The senior cardiologist noticed it too but he continued without letting his attention get diverted.

"An angry mob is waiting for Sir downstairs and they are hitting every hospital staff who is crossing their path. Any moment the gate would collapse and we would have to run for our lives."

"They are hitting the building and breaking down assets," said Sharma.

"Calm down. Sir will not leave this lab until the procedure is over or until there is not a single brick left of this building," said the Incharge.

The procedure continued in silence and perfect attentiveness as if nothing had happened. Shouts and yells could now be heard from inside the catheterization lab as more and more people gathered. Suddenly, the perfect harmony outside the lab was disrupted with a shattering sound followed by that of something rolling on the floor. A large stone had broken in through the windowpanes in the lobby outside the lab. But they went on with their service with devotion and perseverance.

Senior cardiologist, Dr. Sunil exhaled heavily in relief. The procedure was successful. He ordered the Incharge to keep the patient in ICU for post-procedural care. Few staffs were waiting outside the lab for the surgery to get over. As soon as the patient was taken away from the room, they barged in.

"Sir, please come out fast. We will escort you through the back door. We will take you safely out to the parking. Come with us fast."

"First, let me see what has happened," said the doctor and walked up to the broken window. The staffs repeatedly warned him from behind but he was determined and his word was final. Nobody had the courage to speak against him.

He peered down through the broken window. Almost fifty men and women had assembled below, in front of the entrance gate. They were enraged and shouted, yelled, threw stones and bricks at the hospital building, smashed anything and everything belonging to the hospital that came in their hands. His head reeled and face turned red. But the thing that troubled and traumatized him the most were the jeers and taunts, catcalls and bad-mouthed words calling him names. He could not tolerate it any longer. Drops of perspiration flowed down his forehead and he felt the numbness in his feet return again, years after the biggest trauma in his life.

Someone from the crowd accidentally looked up and spotted him. He became startled as the man alerted the crowd. Many people started to look up one by one. Within moments the agitation in the crowd was in frenzy as they had spotted their target. He could not move as he was overwhelmed with the sprays of stones and metals that started to come up his way. A stone hit him hard in the head and he stumbled. The staff came rushing and steadied him. Blood had tainted his white coat.

They took him inside and seated him on a chair. He hung his head closing his eyes for a few moments of absolute silence as his team waited with bated breath for a word to escape his mouth, ready to carry out any command. He finally raised his head.

"Leave this room for the time being," he said calmly.

"But Sir…they are—"

"I command. Leave me alone for some time. Please…" he followed his command with a request as he knew his men loved and respected him.

They started to leave the room one by one looking back every time they reached the door to check if their Sir was alright.

Everyone was gone. The shouts and yells had increased by leaps and bounds. Few more stones and varied objects flew in through the windows breaking some more glass panes. The man arose from the table and walked calmly to the door. He closed it and returned to the table. He picked up a scalpel from the table and held it up to his eyes. The jeers and catcalls no longer seemed to disturb him. His feet ceased to feel numb. His mind was made up.

ONE

IN SEARCH OF GOD

The dark sky rumbled above like the growl of a thousand drumbeats and far beneath, a solitary pair of light beams sped on slicing the blue-grey darkness in two, splitting through the wheat fields on either side. To the other side of the growing layers of murky clouds the sun was yet not set beyond the horizon, but the pouring afternoon beneath the dark heavens hastily yielded to an early nightfall, a little too early. The clouds had been layering up in the sky since midday, but they never rained for once until now and the showers erupted in a blinding deluge.

Rain lashed the windowpanes. Sam pulled out the hands-free from his ears to listen to the rainy monotone of an alien land. Soil and dry earth that had accumulated on the windscreen travelling through the parched, dusty roads of Rajasthan dispersed in circular shapes with curious serrated edges as large drops of rain landed upon it with force.

"We will reach Muradpur in a few minutes," said Ajay.

Sam couldn't hear him due to the deafening sound of the rain lashing the metal top of the car. He kept looking outside through the windows and watched. In the far fields which had a gloomy backdrop of a dark rainy afternoon, scantily clad children ran and danced in the rains. With all its fields, makeshift haylofts standing out solitary here and there in the expanse, children running in glee and trees stooping to the ground tortured by the force of the showers, the village seemed to be melting down and dissolving away in the continuous flow of rainwater rippling and rolling down the windscreen, disappearing somewhere into the roaring engines.

"The network here is very poor. And possibly has even deteriorated due to the heavy rains," said Ajay putting the phone back into his pocket.

This time Sam had heard him and looked back, "Don't we have the exact address?"

"We do, but it is difficult to find a house in these remote villages."

The car came to a halt at the very first sight of a lone man walking through the torrential rains with an umbrella that barely was of any help.

Gusts of cold wind and rain sprayed onto his face the moment Ajay slid down the car window and asked in local Rajasthani, "Can you tell the way to Dr. Sunil's ancestral residence?"

The man didn't respond at first and kept looking at the foreigner with curious eyes. Ajay repeated and the man started reciprocating. Sam only watched the moving lips and gesturing fingers of the man as he said the direction to their destination. The windowpane slid back up and the car sped away from the man slowly disappearing behind in the haze of the rains.

Sahiram was going to lean back on the *chaupahiya* that had just been dragged inside from the open porch, when he heard the voice of Jairam, his younger brother, calling from the gates, "Bhaisahab… someone has arrived from *videsh,* and he wants to talk to you."

Sahiram reluctantly rose from his stance and slid his feet into his slippers. He came out till the shaded area of the porch. A white car waited just outside the half-opened gates with its screen wipers in motion, the headlights on and engines roaring. The water accumulated inside its headlight casing rippled with the motion of the vibrating engine. Two men were standing at the gates with Jairam who was offering them an umbrella.

"I am Ajay," the Indian of the two men spoke out opening the umbrella, "I was sent by Dr. Abhishek from UK to assist Mr. Sam to write a biography on Dr. Sunil. We will be obliged if you could kindly spare some of your time to tell us something about Dr. Sunil."

Ajay was going to continue when Sahiram interrupted him.

"Wait, wait. Come inside first. We shall talk about it."

The foreigner looked around the massive, old, time-worn building in awe. The women of the household were busy gathering and collecting their *challahs* and other kitchen belongings and taking them inside the shed.

As the men went inside, the engine stopped roaring and the headlights went off.

"First, tell me why you want to write a… a…"

"A biography," prompted Ajay.

"Yes, right. What is it and why do you want to write it?" asked Sahiram leaning back on a wooden chair after the two men were seated properly first.

Jairam managed another chair from somewhere inside and sat down on it beside Sahiram.

"Mr. Sam here, has come in search of some tales that will inspire. He first went to the famous doctor in his native country, Dr. Abhishek, for such a story, but he said 'If you mean inspiration then you haven't come to the right place; who else's life could be more inspiring than that of Dr. Sunil?' and advised Mr. Sam to go to India and visit Dr. Sunil's ancestral home in Muradpur. So, here we are. We have come a long distance. We have come here to know about Dr. Sunil, his life and his childhood that was spent here. Even a little something would suffice, Sir. It's a request," Ajay said earnestly.

A pin drop silence prevailed for few minutes. Only the laborious droning sound of frogs croaking came in from the water bodies that had been created in several places in and around the yard by the rainwater.

Sahiram cleared his throat and sat up erect. His eyes focused on nothing but the infinity, giving the impression of the time travel he had already set off in his mind.

"I was working in the post of a Platoon commander in the RAC (Rajasthan Armed Constabulary). My brother Jairam managed and looked after our farms in the village. I don't exactly remember the year, but I do remember those times. One sixteen-year-old boy had the whole nation cheering for him. Whenever he walked into the twenty-two yards of the cricket field, the gallery would erupt screaming his name. He left us amazed and inspired hundreds and thousands of children throughout the country. My children never told me explicitly but perhaps they too had looked up to that sixteen-year-old boy who proved that nothing is impossible...be it the battleground or the playground."

"Around 1989," Jairam prompted.

"Yes, could be. My memory is diminishing..." he continued after a pause. "I was away at work posted at Sriganganagar when I received a letter from home. It only said 'the fruitages are going bad. Come home soon.' You all know how important the crops are for a farmer's household. So, I instantly packed my bags and set out for home. Many of my colleagues forbade me to travel suddenly without prior notice and application but I knew the harvests were only two and a half months away and if I did not return in time, we were going to have a bad year ahead..."

⚜

It was the time of sundown and a color of molten gold was spread all over across the far stretched fields. Sahiram was walking across the fields towards his home, his weary hands and shoulders weighed down by luggage, when he spotted the sight of the children playing at a distance. The scene rippled in the heat wave that the scorched earth gave off at the end of the day. Yet he didn't have a difficulty recognizing the figures from afar; Anil, Sunil and Rajvir.

"There arrives the 'flying'! There arrives the 'flying'! C'mon, let's hide! Let's run!" he could hear the tallest boy laughing and shouting. The younger boys looked at his direction and one of them shot out from the group and came running to him.

"Baba run, run, let's hide somewhere, the 'flying' has arrived."

Sunil held Sahiram by the hand and started dragging him. Anil, the boy who was shouting till now came and struck lightly at the back of his younger brother's head.

"Are you silly? He is the one, he is the 'flying'," he said, pointing to Sahiram.

All of the rest laughed out loud. Sahiram lifted Sunil in his arms and gently twisted the other boys' ears in mock anger. The boys then picked up his luggage and they all departed towards the direction of the setting sun, as their frames casted tapered, elongated shadows trailing behind them through the grassy fields.

Dusk had fallen. A little mud lamp was humbly gleaming along the edge of the porch. Two kerosene lamps burned bright near the two women who sat in the open front yard; one with an array of chopped vegetables and the other with a *chullah* in front of her. Urns, pitchers and large cooking vessels lay stacked around them. They were talking to each other in raised voices. At a little distance Jairam was relaxing in a half-lying posture on a *chaupahiya*. A little radio sat on the ground near him and blurted out local songs and news in intermittently cracking voices, perpetually accompanied by a coarse, grating noise in the background.

The uproar of the children made everyone turn their heads and look towards the gate. As soon as they saw Sahiram enter with the three boys carrying his baggage, there was a dead silence for a moment. The two women shot up to their feet and drew the *saree* over their heads. Jairam jumped up lowering his legs from the *chaupahiya* to the ground and hurriedly switched the radio off. He then rushed to Sahiram and took the baggage from him.

"Bhai Sahab, you didn't inform that you were coming," asked Jairam, baffled.

"Sorry, I didn't get you. You informed Shanti about our crops going bad, didn't you? That's why I received a letter calling me back," replied an equally baffled Sahiram.

"Crops going bad? No, why would I say like that? We are going to have a fine harvest this coming winter. What has happened?" Jairam retorted in total confusion.

Sahiram analyzed the situation for few moments and then replied calmly, "Nothing *chhote*."

Jairam looked with unsatisfied perplexity as Sahiram went up to the enormous pitcher kept at one corner of the porch. The children were running about the yard despite repeated admonition by the two women busy in their chores. Sahiram tried to ignore them initially when all of a sudden, a piece of eggplant came in flying, hitting Sahiram in the shoulder, accompanied by an iterating sound of metal striking the hard, stony ground.

Sahiram looked back. Rajvir stood terrified with his one foot placed in an urn turned over on its one side and pieces of vegetables strewn around it. Another saucer went rolling ahead like a tire towards the gate. Sahiram walked towards a frightened Rajvir. He closed his eyes half expecting a blow to land on him.

"Go bring back the plate first and then sit on haunch holding your ears as your punishment."

Rajvir went ahead thanking the gods for lessening his punishment as the other two boys sullenly tried to slip out of the scene.

"Where are you going? Come here and join Rajvir," Sahiram equally reprimanded his own boys, Anil and Sunil.

The surroundings started to fill with the aroma of freshly cooked, steaming meals. The food was simple yet delicious by virtue of the care and devotion with which they were prepared. Sahiram and Jairam sat down on the cloth spread out on the porch as Shanti Devi and Jairam's wife started serving.

"What was it about the fruitages going bad, Shanti?" asked Sahiram in a muffled tone as his wife hunched forward to serve on his plate. Shanti continued to serve without giving a reply. "I am asking something," Sahiram looked in her eyes.

"Three months back, when I wrote to you about my ill health and asked you to come home, you didn't come then. And now you are coming just on the mention of your crops going bad. Don't you care about anything else apart from the crops?" said Shanti in a voice heavy with complaint.

Sahiram heaved a sigh in annoyance but contained himself, "I see that the fruitages are all right. You better had not lied to me about all this."

"No, they are not and I didn't lie. I was not speaking of the fruitages growing on The fields; I was speaking of these fruitages growing up in our homes. Sometimes do take notice of your kids also," Shanti gestured with her eyes towards the punished children sitting in a corner behind the water pitcher.

Sahiram became thoughtful looking at the farthest nothing for a few moments and then he looked back at the children.

"Come up here. Sit down quietly and have your supper," he said sternly trying to hide the merciful kindness reflected in his eyes. The children came up one by one and sat down before Sahiram as the women continued to serve.

⁂

The sun belonging to the sky arose from behind the hills with the promise of a new day. But the millions of suns that rise each day on the mothers' foreheads often rise even before the sun belonging to the skies. Shanti was up before the sun had risen. She rolled up her mat from the ground and looked once at the sleeping children. She would prepare the breakfast before anyone else in the family would open their eyes. And then she would wake the children up for school.

This was a regular morning at the household. A lunch carrier box for each of the family members was kept ready at the porch. Larger ones were for the men who would work day long in the fields and smaller ones for the children. Sahiram and Jairam stood near the pitcher in the front yard chewing and rubbing on their teeth a neem branch each.

The children were almost ready for school when Sunil slowly walked up to his mother and stood silently by her watching her do her chores.

"The food is ready at the porch. Take it yourselves. I have a lot of work here. Don't ask me to put them in your bags now," said Shanti assuming her son's expectations.

"Maa, get me married."

Shanti looked up, astounded. Then collecting her wits, she replied, "Should I tell your father, that you wish to get a good beating? Is this an age for getting married? Huh? Go fast now. You are getting late for your school."

An impatient Rajvir called from outside the gates, "How longer will you take to make a groom out of yourself? Come fast, we are getting late."

"Maa, get me married. I have seen how to get married at a friend's wedding ceremony. She dropped out of school. And whatever I see for once I remember it perfectly. I can't watch you work so hard for all of us that you don't even get a proper night's sleep. If my bride comes, your work will get shared. You won't have to wake up before the sunrise."

"Yes, you're right. Another child will come to run about and play around the house! Go fast now," reprimanded his mother.

Sunil slowly went out racking his brain to find other solutions to the situation.

The school was over a mile away, crossing the borders of the village, in a nearby town. They would always run for the school yet they would be late as every other day. It was a single storied building painted with cheap, bright orange paint having navy blue doors, windows, borders and pillars. The prayers in chorus voices could be heard from outside the gates. Anil went a story up towards his own classroom in the eighth standard. The rest moved inside the ground floor corridor and pushed the dark blue door of their classroom.

"Now, there arrive the gems of Muradpur. And what excuses do you have to tell me for today?" reprimanded the teacher primarily targeting Rajvir, known as the notorious among the two.

"Do not scold him Sir, today all of us came late because of me. I was asking my mother to get me married so that my bride can help her in her chores, but she rebuked me. I was trying to think of some other ways to convince her to get me married, throughout the journey from home to school, which also slackened my pace. I am sorry Sir," said Sunil hanging his head as the rest of the classroom broke out in laughter.

"This is why Sunil, this is exactly why you are a beloved child despite all your mischiefs. Always be like that, honest from the core and you will go a long way in life." He then looked back at Rajvir. "Go and sit on the first bench the two of you and pay attention. If I see any mischief on your part, you will not get another chance and will have to stand outside for the rest of the school hours today. No other teacher will come to your rescue and I will make that sure."

They quietly sat down in perfect harmony and watched the teacher write the word "Bhagwan" on the board. The teacher turned back and asked the class, "Tell me whom do we call Bhagwan, a God?"

"Only God knows what is going to happen to these unruly children," remarked Sahiram regretfully while taking out the lunchboxes out of the tote bag, to Jairam who were now sitting at the side of the footwalk beside the fields to have their meal.

The teacher continued the explanation quoting few lines from the sacred *Pandav Gita* and the *Mahabharata*.

"Twameva Mata Cha Pita Twameva, Twameva Bandhushcha Sakha Twameva,

Twameva Vidya Dravinam Twameva, Twameva Sarvam Mama Deva Deva"

The lines written in blocked Devnagari were glowing brightly against the black board. "What do we learn from these lines?" again asked the teacher trying to explain it to the children. "In these lines, that "someone" is given, at first, the ranks of a mother and a father, then the ranks of a truthful real friend and guide, then the ranks of true knowledge and capital or materials that help sustain our livelihood. And lastly, He is revealed as the 'everything', the God of all Gods. So, we learn that God Himself is being compared to a mother and father and since He is being given the ranks of the parents, He becomes a supreme God, the God of all Gods, the 'everything' of all things. So now tell me how we can please the Gods who are so near us?"

"By studying hard."

"By taking care of them."

"By listening to all that they ask us to do."

"By regarding our parents as our God."

Varying answers came from all over the classroom. A lanky hand went up in the air with lots of questions brimming in his eyes.

"Yes, Sunil?" prompted the teacher.

"Sir, in the second line God has been compared to true knowledge and the capital or materials to sustain ourselves. All of these come directly or indirectly from a teacher. So, if knowledge gets to be compared with God and the means of our sustenance too, then the giver of that knowledge, the guide who helps us to grow up and earn our sustenance, the teacher could also be compared to God, so you too are God, isn't that right, Sir?"

"Yes, you could say that," replied the teacher, a little embarrassed and trying to keep a low profile in front of the class yet nodding in assertion, smiling inwardly appreciating the analyzing powers and philosophical maturity of the young boy.

Then to end the embarrassing silence, he found a brilliant idea. "You could also call a doctor a God. Whenever we face some danger in life we pray to God, right? Whenever we are faced with life threatening problems then too, we pray to God. Now think, a doctor saves our lives from life threatening situations, he is the one who answers to all those prayers we make to God in those times. So shouldn't he be called God as well?"

"Yes Sir, Yes Sir," erupted the classroom. Only Sunil was too engrossed and mystified to say anything.

The day was about to be over. The sun had inclined to the west and the shadow of the neem tree in the play yard of the school gradually grew towards the east, becoming more elongated and tapered. The children waited for the final bell to call it a day. Sunil patiently watched the shadow move.

Rajvir asked from behind, "What are you watching so intently?"

"See Raju, see the shadow move!" said Sunil enthusiastically.

Rajvir looked at it for some moments but then retired saying, "I can't see anything moving. You could only see it after it has moved quiet a distance perceptible to human vision."

"But what is the benefit of noticing something after it has already occurred, neither will you be able to control it, stop it nor learn something from it. I can see it. You just have to still yourself and watch with patience so that the vision could grow sensitive to even a little movement which is otherwise invisible."

"Continue. You have your useless time and patience to use up somewhere, we don't." And he left.

Sunil was amazed to discover that with a little patience and attention to detail one can see things that many persons can't.

The earth was scorched and immensely heated up absorbing the sun's rays throughout the day. Anil walked ahead wearing a shoe, Sunil a floater and Rajvir ran behind naked feet, trying to catch up with them. Their figures rippled in the heat waves coming out from the scorched earth.

"Ae Sunil, drop your *chappal,*" shouted Rajvir from behind as he tottered on the burning earth.

Sunil reached a tree shade and threw his floaters towards Rajvir. Rajvir slid his feet into them. After walking a few hundred feet, Sunil asked it back. Rajvir stood below a tree shade and threw it back to Sunil. In this way when they had come in front of "Bodan ka Pahad", the floaters were in Rajvir's feet. This was Sunil's favorite playground. Whenever in their journey they encountered the "Bodan ka Pahad", they would never leave it without competing in a race from its foot to peak and back to foot. Sunil would invariably win each time.

"Watch Sunil, the *chappal* is in my feet. Let's see how you win today."

This was a challenge Sunil would never turn down without a fitting reply. They all moved back at their decided mark and started running. Sunil knew the earth would tingle, sting and cause burning blisters onto his feet. He readied his mind for the expected and let go. The three boys ran with all their might. Breeze ruffled through their hair. The afternoon sun blazed bright. But they ignored it all. Their eyes were fixed on the peak. They had played this game many times, yet it never grew old. Each time the challenge was taken up as enthusiastically as always.

Different seasons of going up and coming down. And finally came the moment of truth. Yes, Sunil it was. He had won it this time too. He could now feel the brunt of it in his sole. Large blisters had appeared under his feet. But then again, it was fun, exhilarating and boosted his confidence. Whenever he faced a challenge in life, he would remember how he prepared himself for the worst even knowing in his heart that he would invariably win. It would be a forever boost for him.

The gates, like always, were wide open. The children barged in. The first thing they always expected after returning from school was a full plate of *RotiSubzi* kept in covered vessels for each of them, on the porch. They ran towards the porch with hunger burning in their stomach. But the porch was disappointingly empty.

"Maa! Maa!" They shouted in unison as they broke in through the half-closed door of the building. The inside was dark as netherworlds.

"Speak low. Do not shout. Mother is ill," scolded Sahiram.

As their visions adjusted to the darkness inside, they saw Shanti lying on the floor on a mattress. Sahiram was attending to her. Sunil came and sat beside his mother.

"What happened, maa?"

"Nothing much. It's only a little fever. I have prepared your favorite chutney. Go and ask *chhoti* maa."

"Sunil, have something quickly and go to the doctor's chamber and bring him home," commanded Sahiram.

⁕⁂⁕

A long queue had built up in front of the single room chamber. The queue could be seen from afar. It came out of the room and had curled up round its backyard in meandering lines to fill up all the space in the courtyard. Sunil headed straight for the man issuing the serial numbers and taking payments. As he entered the room, he saw another parallel queue emerging beside the longer one. It was much shorter and ended after ten to twelve persons. Sunil went and stood in the shorter queue.

"Ae boy… Do you have change money? If you do, stand there, otherwise join this queue outside."

"Yes. I have," said Sunil confidently though he knew he had no money with him at all since he came to take the doctor with him. His charges would be paid at home by his father.

He looked around. It was a puny room with thatched roof and mud walls. A makeshift hay barrier provided a little privacy to the part of the doctor's chamber. But a little square hole serving as the window did not have any cover. Sunil at one point stood just beside the window as the queue moved forward. He looked inside.

"Only you can do something, Doctor Saab. He has immense faith in you. He knows you will make everything alright. It is with this faith he still smiles today despite all the pain and suffering in his body. You are a God to him…and to all of us," a woman was speaking, standing with her back to the window.

Sunil had learned something today at his school. He always thought that knowledge could be found in books. But today his teacher had taught him true knowledge. Now he realized that true knowledge could be found everywhere in practical life and is not confined to schoolbooks. He got a real example of what his teacher taught them today. Doctors were truly Gods in disguise! He smiled in his mind as this realization settled in him.

"Ae, aren't you Sahiram's son?" asked the doctor when he spotted him peeking inside.

"Yes, doctor saab," replied Sunil, a little frightened for being caught red handed, looking inside.

"Come in. What has happened?"

Sunil boldly went in while giving a puffed-up, side-cast look to the man collecting payments.

"Doctor saab, my mother is very ill, she couldn't come here. Baba has sent me to take you home."

"Ohh…come along. Let's see what has happened to your mother," he said as the woman left the chamber.

The doctor handed Sunil his bag and instruments and seated himself on his bicycle. He looked back and said, "What are you looking at? See, you must not ride on it. Walk ahead in front of me. I will follow you."

Sunil did as was asked. Suddenly something irked inside him. He looked back and asked the doctor innocently, "The\y say doctors are Gods. Is it so? Are you a God?"

The man stopped moving his paddles and looked at the boy who had asked this blatant question on his face, for a moment. "Come. Sit behind me," was the answer he could muster.

Sunil walked down and climbed clumsily onto the back of the bicycle and the two figures rode away into the twilight fields of red and gold.

"It is only a fever from cold. There's nothing to worry about. I am giving a few medicines. Make sure they are taken timely. The fever will be gone in a couple of days."

As the doctor went out and Sahiram followed him outside for his payment and to see him off, Sunil came and sat down by his mother's side.

He put one hand on Shanti's forehead and said, "Maa, I wish to tell you something. I want to be a doctor someday. I want to treat the people and save their lives."

Shanti smiled with some effort and retorted, "Sure, son. Be a doctor and when the day comes you will do the treatment whenever I am ill."

Sunil had taken the charge of the medicines and made sure his mother took them at the right intervals. Sahiram could see something else in this young boy of twelve. But he was yet to be amazed.

Sunil had to leave his mother's side in the morning despite his wishes. Sahiram made sure his children never missed a day at school and any tutor's classes. Sunil used to attend his class teacher's private classes. But he had some other interest too. His tutor had a television at his home. He would finish up all the studies and the day's work in half an hour and keep aside another half an hour for watching television.

Sunil and Rajvir knocked on the newly painted, glossy, green door of their tutor's home.

"We are not late, Sir," Sunil said enthusiastically.

"And why would you be? I know that you have come here for watching the television," the teacher said patting lightly on the back of boys' heads in mock anger. "Go sit inside quietly."

The teacher too had a dilemma. He could not ask the boys to do more as others took the whole one hour to do what Sunil completed in half an hour. It was his credit. He deserved what he wished for. As always, Sunil finished the studies and tasks given by the teacher in just half an hour.

"Sir, may I go and watch the television now?"

"Yes… of course. Who could stop you now?" said the teacher shaking his head in mock despair.

Sunlight infiltrated through the ruffling leaves of the peepul tree that had grown hugging the south wall of the building.

The sun had inclined to the southern sky. Few days were left to *Uttarayan*. The *chaupahiyas* and blankets nowadays were being kept on the southern courtyard instead of the front yard. They would be warmed by the sunrays throughout the day and Sahiram and Jairam dozed off on them during the night. Their slumber used to break with the first rays of the sun falling in through the entangled mesh of leaves and branches of the peepul.

Sahiram blinked open his eyes as the slender beams of sunlight disturbed them. The haze of the fog had yet not cleared completely. Loud yet distant noises of cows mooing came in from the grazing fields that stretched beyond their backyard.

"Babaa! Let's go to the Bodan Mountain and see the sun rise. You missed it though, it's still beautiful," Sunil's voice yelled from somewhere up.

Sahiram looked upward opening his eyes wide. Sunil was bending over from the edge of the roof. It had been many a day, rather many a month that Sahiram hadn't visited the roof top for once.

Without waiting for Sahiram Sunil vanished from the roof and within a few minutes shot out through the door.

Sahiram got up in a mess from the *chaupahiya* and tried to keep pace far behind Sunil. Within five minutes he was already there climbing the rocky mountain slope with dexterity. The scarlet rays of the new sun flooded the crop fields all around. Sahiram slowly came upon the hill tottering behind. After a while he managed to hold Sunil by the hand to drag him away. But he wouldn't listen. He wished to spend some more time in the moment.

"Baba, can't we stay here a little longer in the open?"

"Yes, we can stay in the open but not here. We will go to our terrace. I haven't gone there for so many days. Will you not let me see it?" was Sahiram's wise reply.

And then Sunil was excited to take his father to the terrace of his house. He had made so many wall arts and paints on the terrace walls that he wanted to show his father for a long time. But the repeated requests could never make him come to the roof once. But today his father himself was asking to take him there. His happiness knew no bounds and they headed straight to their terrace after reaching home and what Sahiram saw there on the walls blew his mind away.

'A mother is the God who brings us into this world'

'A father is the God who protects us in this world'

'A teacher is the God who guides us in this world'

'A doctor is the God who lets us live for a second time sometimes even overruling the fate ordained by the Gods'

'The God of all Gods; my everything: Twameva Sarvam Mama Deva Deva'

The walls of the roof were throbbing with vibrant words and phrases inscribed and painted.

Sahiram turned around.

"Look around, Mr. Sam. Here you will get everything you came looking for."

He watched as Mr. Sam went around the wall paintings and inscriptions, now covered by years of soot and moss, faded by the sun rays, yet not entirely perished. They were as visible and legible as they were on the day years ago when Sunil had called Sahiram to the rooftop to watch the sunrise.

"Do you know Mr. Sam, that child labor is a crime in our country?" asked Sahiram sincerely.

"Yes, I do, and why only in India? It is a crime all over the world; morally if not legally."

"Yes, Sir. But sometimes we do this crime knowingly, completely aware of the unethical grounds it has. Nobody will ever know what poverty is unless they have sometimes in their life experienced it themselves. The educated world will continue judging us. There will be legal laws and campaigns to prevent child labor, child marriage and other similar morally unethical issues. But when it comes to filling your bellies at the end of the day even educated people turn selfish and brutish…I became too.

"It was a year of opulent harvests after two years of poor fruitage. There was nothing except the hopes of good income in the coming year after we could send out the crops to the market. But to take them to the market, labors are needed. Due to the poor harvesting in the preceding two years, we had not enough money to arrange for laborers. Our children continued to help us despite their sincerity in studies, carrying the sacks of vegetables and grains on their strong young shoulders, loading and unloading the carts for the markets. But sometimes it would become too much for the young boys and they looked for excuses to evade doing it. I watched them carrying the heavy sacks bending them to the ground, I knew how it weighed down their young shoulders. I wished to tell them 'Leave it son…you have other dreams to go after. Leave it to us,' but I knew I couldn't say that. Then one day came and I was posted to Jaipur. I moved to the city with my children after completion of their high school."

Mr. Sam looked away towards the East. The clouds of the last night's rain had all drifted away. The sun was rising with its scarlet spread all over the quiet village of Muradpur.

TWO

CHASING DREAMS

Mr. Sam took out a notebook from his bag. Until this time he was only listening to Sahiram but never attempted to take down any notes, but now he knew what was coming. He knew it very well too. It was part of his life too; it was his most favorite part. As he held the pen and paper his hand trembled a little, remembering how they occurred in his own life at different points of time; what their incredible driving power were; they could make a person achieve unbelievable feats, travel unconceivable distances. These powerful elements, they are called dreams.

Sahiram continued, "After my posting to Jaipur I had been provided a rented one room flat in the city. My children had forever traveled long distances in order to get anything in life, even for a little preliminary education. I had made up my mind that they wouldn't have to suffer in silence anymore. So, I decided to take them along with me to the capital and complete the rest of their studies there."

✦

Shanti stuffed as much as she could in the bags of three children.

"Maa. How many more meals are you going to pack? Ladoos are available in the cities too. Now this bag has become as heavy as the other baggage if not more."

Shanti did not pay heed. Mothers are only ever concerned about how much can be stuffed for their children to eat.

Three tin trunks and a large cotton cloth containing several odd miscellaneous items fastened with knots formed between each diagonally opposite pair of ends were ready at the front yard near the gate. Shanti put down another bag full of foodstuffs. Sunil, Anil and Rajvir took up their respective trunks and waited for Sahiram at the gates.

They had planned to set off early in the morning and take the first bus towards the city. But now the sun was already up in the sky. The growing heat could be felt. Shanti had packed enough water that made the food baggage much heavier than usual. Sahiram came with a cotton towel and headed towards the large barrel of water kept at the corner of the front yard. He soaked the towel in water and came to Shanti.

"I hope you have taught these monkeys how to cook and look after the household," then looking at the children he said, "This is the last day you are getting delicious, cooked meals ready at your disposal. Take all you can. And be thankful to your mother."

The sun shone bright in the sky. Sahiram looked up and estimated the time they would take to reach the bus stand. Swiping his face and ears once with the wet towel he left with the children. Shanti stood at the gates and watched on. The four figures with trunks swinging from their hands slowly diminished in the golden fields. With every swing of their hands the sun reflected from the tin trunks and dazzled Shanti's eyes. Even after they had travelled a long distance ahead Shanti still stood at the door. She could see them no more but the sun light kept on dazzling her eyes at a constant interval from far and farther away.

✦

"Here, hold this." Sahiram asked Rajvir to hold his sack for a moment while he searched his personal belongings for the keys.

It was pitch dark everywhere. Crickets chirped in a lingering monotone. Gongs of temple bells sounded faintly from somewhere far away behind the backyard of the old building.

"The landlord never lets us keep the staircase lights on. He had cut the electricity lines from here. Such a miser," exclaimed Sahiram, with regret.

"Take out the torch. Who has it?" asked an impatient Rajvir.

"Yes, just a minute." Sunil threw himself down on the ground with his trunk and opened it up wide. Then without rummaging through the stuffs he quickly took it out.

"Can you see in this darkness too?" asked Anil.

"No. I remembered exactly where I had put it. And once I had seen it there, there's no chance I would forget." Sunil promptly replied.

Sahiram had taken out the keys with the help of the torch. As he put the keys into the keyhole he said addressing all the boys, "Look around carefully and take notice of everything around. Know this place well. The coming times are going to be spent in here. Maa won't be here to cook your meals and neither would be Chacha to take care of you monkeys. So, understand things and learn to take care of yourselves and the household."

The boys and Sahiram entered the room. A stuffy smell of damp mattresses and pillows mixed with a sweet musky aroma of wooden furniture was filled up inside the room.

A week had passed by since they settled in their new home. A cloth was spread on the floor. Anil and Sunil were carrying the meals from the kitchen and Rajvir was placing the plates before everyone's seat. It was late in the night since Sahiram had extended duties. The boys waited for him.

"So, what the three of you have decided finally?" asked Sahiram as he washed his hands and came to sit down before his plate.

"Baapu, I want to attempt PMT once more. I have already started preparing for that," said Anil excitedly.

"Look, Anil. You have already attempted PMT once last year. Neither do I have the patience nor the money to continue your studies any longer. This is your final chance. If you can't make it go back to village and start working in the farms with your Chacha." Sahiram remarked seriously.

Anil lowered his head disheartened. Sunil paused eating for a moment and started thinking, looking blankly at the floor. Rajvir kept on stuffing into his mouth. Sahiram tore a piece from his *Fulka* Chappati and while dunking it into the *daal* asked Sunil without looking at him, "And what about you Sunil? Tell me what you are thinking?"

"Baapu, I think I am going to reattempt my 12th in mathematics."

Sahiram was going to put the piece of *fulka* dipped in *daal* into his mouth but paused to look at Sunil in bewilderment. "Have you gone nuts? You passed your 12th in Bio with good marks, so why is this idiocy of reattempting it?"

"Baapu, you just said that I have only one chance to attempt PMT. And I don't have any plans to go back to village and manage the farms, ever. So even if I can't become a doctor at least I would become an engineer. That is why I want to reattempt mathematics."

Anil looked at Sunil dumbfounded. Even Rajvir stopped eating to look at Sunil.

"Look, Sunil. I don't have any doubt in your capabilities. Only, I just have enough money to help you attempt only once. Whatever you want to do, think it out properly before doing. Did you get me?"

"Yes Baapu, and there's one more thing to say."

"Tell me."

"Alongside 12th reattempt in mathematics I will also prepare for PMT and NDA as well. I will clear and get selected at least in any one or the other."

"I had no doubts that you are out of your mind, but I just came to know today that you are entirely mad. People struggle to clear one and here you are expecting to attempt all three together at a time. Just do the reattempt without another word," Sahiram said in an admonishing tone.

"No, Baapu. I have decided in my mind. And please don't worry or get tensed, I can do this. I have to take this the way I take the challenge of 'Bodak ka Pahad', I have understood this."

"What does 'Bodan ka Pahad' have anything to do with this?" Rajvir asked innocently.

"Rajveerey, forget about 'Bodan ka Pahad', tell me what you are going to do?" asked Sahiram with faking a smile at Rajvir.

"I don't plan, Baapu. Rajvir will follow wherever *bhaiya* Sunil goes. I will also start preparing for PMT along with my brothers."

Sahiram looked at all three for few moments and then said addressing all, "Whatever you do make sure you do that well and another important thing is you must be your own mother in here. Because there will be no one to prepare meals four times a day for you. So alongside doing your studies divide the cooking, cleaning and other household chores among yourselves. You know I can't just leave my service to start serving you." Sahiram stood up to clean his hands and walked towards his room.

As Sahiram disappeared into his room Anil jabbed Sunil with his elbow, "Have you gone really mad, Sunil? Listen to me, concentrate on PMT. I have studied for one year and this time too I will study. I will explain your things and studying together all three of us will clear it this time. Trust me."

"Bhai, selection has to happen. But the problem is Baapu doesn't have enough money that he can afford our coaching classes over and over. I have only one chance. I shall definitely crack at least one or another."

"Over confidence is not a good thing, Sunil. Listen to me," warned Anil.

"Bhai saab, just have a little faith in me. Sunil can do this," Sunil said gloriously as he calmly retreated into his room.

The next few months went by in strict routine for the kids. They would cleverly divide their time in studying and doing the chores. They did not study too hard but maintained a strict regularity and routine in whatever they did. That was the reason they got to play and do household chores even after spending satisfying hours after studying. Sahiram would many times spot the light glowing in the kids' room in the middle of the night and a muffled chorus tone would come from the inside. Sometimes he would come back from work and see the kids studying. These months thus passed by and then one day came the moment of truth.

"And what were the outcomes?" Mr. Sam asked excitedly.

"That day I left from my work as soon as I had received the news. My workplace was not too far away from and yet not too close to where I lived. I was trying to walk fast avoiding the traffic, but it slowed down my pace over and over. Finally, I had reached our home and ran up the stairs in the hope of giving the surprising news to my children as soon as I entered. I knocked on the door repeatedly, but no one opened it. I was growing a little tensed. So, I fetched the spare keys from the landlord and entered. There was not a sound coming from their room.

I opened it gently. Anil was lying on the floor with his book on top of his face. Rajvir had made a pillow of his books and Sunil's book was shut close by his side, he too was sleeping soundly. All the three were sleeping like a log. They had no idea of their victories."

⁂

"Hey boys! Get up," Sahiram shouted.

All the three agitated and quickly became alert of Sahiram's presence. They started making up excuses to justify themselves.

"Baapu, I was studying lying down and didn't know when the book fell on my face," said Anil.

Rajvir joined him, "Yes Bapu, I too was studying and had no idea when I dozed off."

"What's the matter Sunil? Tell me now, did you all come here to sleep? Do you have any intention to do something in your life or not?"

"We are sorry, Bapu. Forgive us," Sunil said hanging his head down.

Sahiram smiled and came closer, "Raise your head high, son. This is no time to keep it down. All three of you have cleared PMT! This is the time when the world will bow down to you. You have fulfilled my dreams today. And Sunil, here you go, you have cleared all the three. Today I have no way other than to accept that you can do anything."

Sahiram had already bought sweets on the way home. He hugged the boys and distributed the sweets among them.

"Sit down here. Now the time has come to discuss something really serious; something that will shape your whole life."

The boys sat down on the floor and Sahiram took a chair and seated himself. "What are your plans now, Anil?"

"Bapu, I will take up Dental."

"And you, Sunil?"

"Baapu, I have made up my mind for the Army. Serve the country, just like you."

"Sunil…now you are grown up and mature enough to take your own decisions. But I would recommend that you go for Medical."

"Why is that, Baapu?"

"Because once you go into the Army you won't be able to go for Medical. But if you go for Medical then you can later come into Army as well."

"It's very true," remarked Anil.

Sunil fell into deep thinking but did not say anything. When Sahiram asked Rajvir about his plans he declared to choose the field of medicine since that was all he could do as he had only given PMT.

"I will wait for your decision, Sunil. Let me know what you have decided by tomorrow."

⁂

"The year was 1993 and Dr. Richard J. Roberts and Phillip Allen Sharp had won the noble prize for their studies and discoveries of split genes. It might have been a tremendous boost for my confused Sunil to zero in on Medical as his career, because it came to him as an omen, like an untold path shown by the Gods to him."

⁂

Sahiram was sleeping in his bed. Suddenly he heard Sunil banging the door and calling him. Sahiram arose from the bed and looked at the watch. It was 5.30 in the morning. The sky was still dusky grey. Sahiram went and opened the door. Sunil was standing right outside. He grabbed Sahiram by the arm and dragged him to the children's room.

"Baapu…I have decided. I will go for Medical. I will grow up to be famous doctor like Dr. J Roberts. I will make you proud, Bapu."

"Alright then. Since everybody has decided, now it's time to fill up the admission forms of the colleges of your choice. And from now onwards your Bapu won't be there with you. You will live your life on your own."

The boys' faces turned a little sullen hearing this though they could feel the joy of new beginnings inside. The day came over when Anil had chosen his ways in a dental college of his choice and his ways were going to be different from Sunil and Rajvir. Rajvir had chosen his own medical college according to his rank in the exam and Sunil his own.

⚜

Sunil now was ready to taste the first sip off his cup of dreams. He had arrived at the college premises. It was a Sunday afternoon. The premises were less crowded than other days at this time. His tin trunks and shabby clothes were no match for the glamour and grandeur of the institute. He looked around with fear and apprehension as well as excitement brimming in his heart. Among the lesser crowd few people spotted him and sounds of muffled taunting laughter reached his ears. The gem of

Muradpur had already reached his destination to change his destiny but he had no idea that this was just the beginning; a lot awaited him in the coming times. There were no one else to protect him, he was all on his own.

After reaching the hostel superintendent and taking the key to his stay for the next few years he reached his room and knocked at the door. But it was already open and just as the back of his fingers touched the door it swung back a little. He entered cautiously and saw another boy like him bending over beside the window side bed pushing his tin trunks below his bed and clapping his hands off the dirt.

He turned and saw Sunil entering his room.

"Brother, cheer up. The one who gets in first, gets the window side bed." The boy then extended his hands to Sunil, "Myself Subhash Dhoot."

"Myself Sunil Kumar Garssa."

"Where are you coming from?"

"I am from Muradpur village."

"Same here brother. I too am from farming background."

Sunil did not reply but thought that the boy was a bit too extrovert and talkative. He is going to have trouble sharing room with this guy considering his own introverted nature.

"We are not here to waste our time thinking who got the window and who couldn't. We are here just to keep our eyes on the trophy; like Arjuna eyeing the eye of the fish," he replied after few moments of silence.

Suddenly there was a commotion and laughter just outside their door. They looked back and saw a group of senior students entering the room. They were laughing and making fun of the last few words spoken by Sunil, "Like Arjuna eyeing the eye of the fish…" They made gestures of holding a bow and arrow and targeting it upwards closing one eye, howling and winking together as they laughed among themselves.

"So, let's start kids? Tell us your names first, Arjunas," one of them asked.

"My name is Sunil Kumar Garssa," replied Sunil, a little tensed.

Another one was encircling them while questioning, "Are you coming from the villages?"

"Hey kids. You should call us Sir. Is that a way of talking to your seniors?" said the first one among them scaring both Subhash and Sunil.

"Take their measurements," he ordered the others.

The second boy among them closed in with a measuring tape and started measuring the two boys, taking their measurements and saying it out loud to the others, "Write…chest…36." Everybody else laughed out loud. "Now write down the measurements of the arm…"

The first of the boys snatched the paper from the one writing down the measurements and pinned it down to Sunil's chest. "Here kids, take your measurements and make a uniform for yourselves. The rest here will tell you how it will be made."

Sunil and Subhash looked on without a word as the first guy left the room.

The day was bright. The crowd was much more than the previous day. Subhash and Sunil entered the campus in their uniform as asked by the seniors. The crowd looked at them, few people laughed but didn't pay much attention as if it was very regular for them; once every year. Suddenly they spotted one boy wearing the same costume as them.

"Bhai Sunil, look there. They made him also wear that."

Slowly, few more appeared wearing similar costume and before long they understood that all those wearing that weird costume of red and white stripes belonged to the new batch of first year students. As they entered the main campus, they saw a queue of first year students in the weird costume already line up and singing in chorus,

"Kadam kadam badhaye ja, khushi key geet gaye ja

Ye jindagi hai kom ki kom pe lootaye ja…"

Naveen, the first of the senior boys who came yesterday to their room, pushed through the crowd towards them and they for the first time noticed his name sewed on his coat.

✥

"What are you looking at? Go stand in the queue and sing with pride. Kadam kadam badhaye ja…"

Sunil and Subhash silently joined the queue and started singing matching their melody. They were not familiar with all the words. So, they kept a low profile and frequently watched the group of seniors enjoying the scene.

✥

Sunil and Subhash had their dinner early in the canteen to avoid facing the bunch of seniors again. As they walked through the silent corridor Subhash said,

"Bhai Sunil, had it been my village I would have showed them all."

"What would you have showed?"

"I would have showed them how to behave. They made jokers out of us and made us sing that song in addition to it. Badan Badan badhaye ja."

"It's not badan badan, it's kadam kadam," Sunil laughed and corrected him as they entered their room.

"Yes, whatever it is…Kadam kadam badhaye ja khushi ke geet gaye ja…"

Sunil took his shirt off and came beside Subhash to join in chorus… "Yeh zindagi hai kom ki tu kom pe lootaye ja…"

Suddenly Naveen entered with three other seniors teasing them since they were caught singing the same song that they were made to publicly sing that morning by the seniors.

"Exactly…that's the spirit. Continue… Kadam kadam badhaye ja."

The others started laughing loudly at his teasing taunts. Naveen came in front of them both.

"The Band of Doctors uniform suited you well," he said and the rest of the senior boys again erupted in laughter.

Sunil and Subhash looked at each other not getting what to say. Naveen broke the silence, "Enough! Now just take off this coat. Hand it over to me."

Subhash replied in hesitation, "Boss, just let it be. It was indeed a nice one. We don't want any more confusion for a new one."

To their utter surprise, Naveen takes out a real white coat and hands it over to them. Both Subhash and Sunil were pleasingly surprised. Sunil's eyes gleamed at the very first sight of the doctor's coat. Sunil put forward his hand to hold the coat, but Naveen pulled his hand back.

"This is no ordinary coat that you could just take it like that. Do you know the real intention and motivation of us behind making you first year kids sing that song in chorus? Yes, you could think it was a mere joke or prank. But the real motive behind making you sing that song was that whenever you wear that coat always remember that despite any number of problems, difficulties or confusions in your own life, you must honor the purpose of this coat. From the very moment you have donned this coat that moment onwards you have to always keep going ahead matching your steps. And the most important thing is that you have to do this all with a smile on your face that must never fade. Do you know half the disease of a patient goes right away the moment he sees the assuring smile on a doctor's face, even a terminal patient's longevity can be extended if he is always kept surrounded with positive vibes? A doctor's smiling face is the first step towards creating that positive energy. That is what a doctor's life is. Even our lives do not belong only to us, we take the oath to serve the ailing without any discrimination of caste, creed and social strata."

Sunil and Subhash were dumbfounded by Naveen's inspiring words. The other seniors too had become serious with a slight hint of proud smile at the corner of their lips listening to Naveen's words.

Naveen put forth his hand and let Sunil take the coat. He didn't wear it but placed it on his body to feel the charisma it radiated.

"There's a saying that power always comes with responsibilities and today Sunil was about to get a taste of that responsibility," Jairam said to Mr. Sam.

***

Sunil realized that the coat indeed had its own charm as he looked at himself at the glass panes fitted on the doors of the patients' chambers aligned on both sides of the main hospital's corridor as he walked slowly through it.

Sunil sneaked into the main hospital for the first time wearing the coat to feel it. He was slowly walking through the corridors.

A nurse crossed his path, "Good morning, Doctor saab…" she said and went away.

A strong smell of phenyl mixed with Dettol filled the corridors. He spotted a sweeper cleaning the floors of the corridor. As he gently passed her by, she greeted him, "Ram Ram Doctor saab." Some patients came out of one of the general chambers and greeted him by bowing down their heads. Sunil was utterly surprised and shocked to find that people had suddenly started respecting him and greeted him like never before.

"Sir, a patient's family is making an issue regarding the discharge of the patient. Please come and look into the matter," a nurse came out and took him inside one of the chambers.

"Ram ram doctor Saab," the patient's father greeted him.

Sunil reciprocated back with a slight smile while amused inwardly.

"Doctor Saab, please release this patient. Do you plan to keep him here forever?"

"Look, actually…" he paused looking at the drip bottle hanging beside the patient's bed and followed the channel with his eyes down to the patient's hand. "The drip is alright…" he said faking seriousness on his face.

He then took up the doctor's note slate in his hand and started putting up an act of going through the notes thoroughly. Suddenly it was snatched away from his hands. He looked up. The senior doctor observed him for a few seconds holding the note slate in his hands and then asked, "Which department are you from?"

Sunil panicked and started walking backwards to the door, "No, Sir. I was just passing by. They called me in here, so I thought…" and he sneaked out of the room heaving a sigh of relief.

He was happy and content with today's experience and the fact that he could get out of the scene without much trouble. He was smiling and walking back along the corridor engrossed in looking at his own reflection on the glass panes when suddenly a hand caught hold of his hand and pulled him inside the room. It was a general ward. Many beds lay side by side.

A woman with tearful eyes folded her hands together in front of him. "Doctor saab…Please look at my son. He is not talking at all. Everything was alright this morning and then I don't know what had happened to him. Please do something, Doctor saab. He is my only son. Please save him, Doctor saab. Only you can do that…you can do that saab…Please save him." She then ran back to her son's bed side and tried to wake him up shaking his body violently, "Get up son, say something…"

After a moment she again ran back to Sunil in frenzy, "Please do something, Saab. You are a doctor, you are God; you can do anything. Please save my son." She requested him with folded hands.

Sunil could not think of what he should do. He knew nothing since he was only a first-year medical student who had sneaked into the hospital wearing a doctor's coat. He felt helpless and started to perspire not knowing how to react or what to do, or where to go. The door creaked behind him and he turned instantly.

A nurse came in and went to the bed. She drew the white cloth over the child's face and declared him dead. The few persons standing around the child broke into tears and the woman who was still standing in front of him with folded hands and tearful eyes stumbled and dropped to the floor. Few men rushed to hold her. Sunil did not know if she had fainted because he ran out of the ward the moment he saw the woman stumble.

He was running with all his might, crossing the hospital garden and then the road honking with traffic, towards his hostel. His vision blurred and his knees gave in. He was stumbling and tripping. At the entrance of the hostel campus, he collided with few other students who watched him curiously as his face was sweating profusely. They mouthed few words at him and then went ahead on their way.

Sunil ran and ran until he reached his room. He took off the coat and hung it on the wall and barged into the washroom. He turned open the tap and threw himself down on the washroom floor below the open tap. His face was red and his tears had mixed up with his sweat and the water flowing down the tap. He was panting and he even didn't bother to undress before going into the shower. The white coat that he so much treasured had unknowingly become the reason of his tears on the very first day he had worn it. He closed his eyes and let the streams of water cool down the agitation and suffering going on in his mind. But as soon as he closed his eyes a hand appeared before his closed eyes and drew the white cover over the child's face.

✕⟨❀⟩✕

Their room window faced the east. The early sunrays fell onto Subhash's bed like shafts of light. He was a son of the village and the sun's rays were enough to wake him up. He woke up and started to get ready for the classes and to his surprise saw Sunil still lying on the bed motionless. He bent over his head and checked his closed eyes for few moments. They were shut close and his eye lids did not move. He thought he was sleeping and did not try to wake him up right away but went to the washroom hoping to find Sunil awake after he returned.

"Sunil bhai, get up. It's time, we will be late for the classes."

Sunil did not respond. Subhash came closer and shook him, "Bhai, don't you want to attend the classes today? Get up fast."

Sunil pushed Subhash's hands away and remarked, "You can go, Subhash. I do not have the mood to attend classes today."

Subhash was a little baffled but did not put in much effort to try to analyze the situation nor did he have the time left to ask Sunil. He took his books and went out of the room leaving Sunil alone.

It was well past 12 in the afternoon when finally, Sunil rose from the bed. He went to the washroom and splashed water on to his face. He slowly came out and stood before the white coat hanging from the door hooks.

"All my life I have believed that if I ever got the power like that of Spiderman or Superman I could change the whole world. But when the power was actually with me, I couldn't realize that you aren't any ordinary coat and nor a person wearing you can ever be. Now you shall wait and watch how I gain control over this power of the coat."

✼

Sunil came out of the hostel room and started walking along the corridor pushing the assembled crowd. He had already seen three more batches of Band of Doctors wearing red stripped coats singing "Kadam Kadam badhaye ja." He came and stopped outside a door in the corridor and knocked, "May I come in, Naveen Sir?"

A voice replied from inside, "Who's there?"

"Sir, this is Sunil. Sunil from final year batch. It seems like you have forgotten us a little too early, though you did rag us well in the first year."

"Ohh, yes yes… Come inside please."

Sunil turned the handle and went inside. A melee of books and documents lay strewn on the table. Naveen sat reading some papers and documents. As he turned to close the door he noticed the white coat hanging from the door hooks. "Tell me, Sunil…"

"Boss… The Pre PG results have come out. Which branch are you taking up?"

"Chest and TB… Why? Is anything wrong?"

Sunil kept quiet for a few moments lost in deep thought, "Then you might as well contract TB."

"Yes…that could happen any moment."

"Is it a serious disease?"

"No, absolutely not. TB is treatable. We just need to take medicines and good diet."

"Actually, Subhash was saying that a new doctor in the department died recently."

Naveen smiled wistfully, "Look, Sunil… Life and death has got no guarantee. They can come and go at any moment. But look at that coat and remember the song you sang on the first day…Kadam kadam badhaye ja…" he pointed at the closed door from which it hung, "That coat is always a remembrance of the fact that our lives are no more ours. Sunil, there is a lot of power in this coat, but power comes with equal responsibility. And this responsibility is to uphold the respect and faith in the minds of people for this coat, to never let it down. This is our duty, even if our lives perish while doing it. And it's not only about TB department. There is equal risk of infection in every other department as well, whichever you choose to do your PG in."

⁂

"Time flew by and one day his MBBS was over. These years had taught him many things right from the power of the white coat to the responsibilities that comes with it. It taught him about the importance of a doctor's life and duty. There was power in his hands now without doubt, but it came with risks… risks to life. But that was not going to stop Sunil from going ahead," Sahiram said looking at the graduation group picture of Sunil hanging from the walls with old flaky paint. Mr. Sam arose from his chair and went closer to the wall.

"That's our Sunil, this is the photo of his MBBS graduation," said Sahiram, smiling with pride.

Sam squinted to look closely at the photo. He noticed another photo frame hanging beside it, the picture of two little girls.

"Who are they?" Sam asked gesturing at the picture.

"These are Sunil's daughters," Sahiram replied.

Ajay asked from behind, "So, when did you get Sunil married?"

"A few years back…in 2006. And he chose a bride for himself."

"Who was she?" Ajay asked.

"What is the big deal in that, Ajay? It is just a love marriage." Sam smiled at Ajay and didn't notice the wrath with which Sahiram stared at him.

Ajay gestured Sam to stop saying things like that. Sahiram, understanding the alienation felt by Mr. Sam with the system of this country, swallowed his anger.

"Dear Mr. Sam, just know that a love marriage in this country is nowhere close to what you find in yours…It involves lots of test and turmoil," Sahiram said.

"What does he know about the system here?" Ajay said, "However I will let him know about it. But first tell us, how and where did they meet?"

"Have you gone mad? Children do not discuss such things with fathers in India. If you want to know about this, you may go to Rakesh. He stays in Jaipur. Go and meet him. I am giving you the address. Go and wreck his brains as well," Sahiram laughed.

Sam and Ajay laughed as well.

The white car started with a roar. Ajay opened the door and sat beside the driver.

"Namaste," Sam greeted Sahiram folding his hands in typical Indian way.

"Thank you very much Sahiram Ji for sparing us your precious time. You have given us a matchless story." Ajay thanked Sahiram ji as he handed a little piece of paper with Rakesh's address.

Sahiram ji raised his hands above his head in the gesture of giving blessings, "Don't spare Rakesh easily. Until you have the information to your satisfaction…"

The car drove off leaving behind a cloud of dense, dark, pungent smoke.

"Sam, you can put the glasses up. The villages are very dusty," Ajay advised Sam.

"No. Just let it be." Sam continued to enjoy the village sights, clean, fresh and green from the squall overnight. Pools of water had appeared in many places. Marshes had come up…Few trees lay uprooted here and there and a smell of wet earth intoxicated the air all around. The sky was still lightly overcast.

Suddenly Ajay turned back, "Hey, Sam?"

"Hmm.."

"There is a question in my mind from today morning…"

"Go ahead."

"If you want to write a book on the life of a medical practitioner, why does he have to be set in India?"

"You might not know Ajay, the Indian medical science is the oldest in the world. Ayurveda is a five thousand year old medical system. Pioneers of Ayurveda included Charaka, Sushruta and Jivaka, who invented implantations, grafting of external body parts and performed laparotomy 2500 years ago. Nowadays laparotomy is done if required or seen anything abnormal in abdomen. The world medical science is inspired by India. There was a time when people from countries all over the world like China, Iran and Greece came to the famous Indian University of Takshashila to study Ayurveda, the traditional Indian Medical science. Now tell me…Is there a better place than India?"

Ajay turned back and replied with a smile, "You know so much about my country than I do. You must write this story to let the world and especially the ignorant Indians like us, know about India's glory in medical science."

Sam turned to look outside. The greenery and soft breeze settled his mind. A short green hill sped behind. He took out his diary… *"Even after knowing and seeing so much sometimes it feels like we are ignorant of so many things happening around us. I don't know where this story will take me but up until now this trip to India has been a success. The mental trauma that a young doctor goes through watching deaths, blood, mutilations and pain before being hardened is no less than that of a soldier on the border. Just like him a doctor risks his own life to save another's… just like him he watches human lives perish in front of his eyes… just like him he too tries to save people but fails sometimes. Nobody will ever know the guilt and self-hatred he might go through when he fails to save a life. Just like him a doctor has not weekends or holidays…yet just like a soldier he continues his service uninterrupted so that we stay healthy and heart."*

He closed his diary and put it back inside. Ajay's head inclined to one side as he started snoring. The car sped on through the green, wet fields.

THREE

CONTROLLING THE HEART

The squeaky-clean floor marbles, the fresh flowers in vases, the mild aroma of scented, floating candles in water filled copper basins with flower petals floating in it and the fresh crispness in air invigorated by some mild, classy room freshener established it clearly that the hosts were prepared for the arrival of the foreigner guest well ahead of time.

Sam and Ajay settled down on the sprawling sofa and looked around impressed. Three teacups and a tea pot were waiting on the little oak wood table kept at the center.

Rakesh spoke first, "Sahiram Ji called me today early in the morning and told everything. I know what you have come here for. But to tell you the truth Mr. Sam, I wonder why you chose to write a book about doctors; I sometimes regret that I chose this profession. We put our sweat and blood, days and nights into treating people but it doesn't take a moment for them to hold the collar of the white coat and accuse us," he continued…

I remember the day when I was sitting with Sunil sir in emergency of MB hospital of RNT Medical College. We both belonged to the same area and I was happy that someone from my neighboring village is in the college.

Sunil sir was in second year of his MD (Medicine) and I was in second year of my MBBS.

He got a call from ICU that one patient died and his bystanders were furious and had beaten the doctor and nursing staff of ward. The mob was angry on every hospital employee but were happy with Dr. Sunil, how he saved their patient in emergency due to which patient was improving initially. But the condition got deteriorated after shifting here in ward because of the treatment of duty doctor present here.

Sunil reached there, unaware of the strength and behavior of mob. Yells of male voices came interrupted by spurts of wailing. On entering the room, Sunil saw the patient lying dead and his relatives encircling the doctor at duty. A middle-aged man held the doctor by his collars and shook him throwing accusing words at his face. A younger man stood beside him watching. Suddenly this man looked towards the door and saw Sunil coming.

"Doctor saab has arrived, doctor saab has arrived… leave him *bhaiya*, we shall talk to Doctor Sunil and let him decide the rest." The man strutted across the room to Sunil, "Doctor saab, he killed our patient. We had come to visit him late in the evening and everything was alright, he talked to us. We do not know anything. You saw him in emergency and started treatment. He started improving after shifting here in ICU. When duty doctor present here started his treatment, his condition worsened and he died. What had he done with the patient? Only you can help us now doctor saab, only you can help us." The man folded his hands and went on complaining.

"Leave his collar first," was the tart reply from Sunil thrown at the older man still holding onto doctor's collar. Both the men were a little perplexed at Sunil's unexpected kneejerk response. The command in his tone was authoritative enough to loosen the fists of the man holding on to doctor's collar. Abhishek, one of Sunil's batch mates too had arrived at the spot of the brawl by then.

Sunil went up and took the note slate from the table and examined it carefully.

After a moment's studying, keeping it down on the table, he said, "All the doses and medicines that were given to the patient after I had left was given exactly as I had prescribed. Doctor has no faults of his. If you have to condemn anybody then it is me, not him. Come on, hold my collars. Come, what are you waiting for? Come and grasp my collars…that's all you want to do, right? To blindly condemn people without even trying to understand the situation."

There was a dead silence in the ward. The women stopped crying for few moments and the men stood there hanging their faces in disgrace of their own thoughtless actions.

"Your patient had multiple problems, he was diabetic with renal failure and drunk as well. His organs were not functioning properly without aid and at this stage body often fails to respond to medications; it does not mean the medications were wrong. You can consult any senior doctor of your choice to judge that. Doctor tried his best, every doctor tries best, but human lives are not entirely in our hands. We are no God the way people think."

⋅✽⋅

"I am going abroad after completing my MD. In the west, doctors are treated like prodigies. They work on their own terms unlike in India where we need to work seventeen-eighteen hours a day, in unhygienic environments without proper preventive measures. And yet whenever something goes wrong, doctors are humiliated and insulted in front of the whole world. It takes us eight to nine years to become a doctor. Still, here in this country, we are always taken for granted."

Sunil interrupted him, "It is not like that, Abhishek. Many people come to India for their treatment. They come because they think that the Indian medical system and Indian doctors have one of the best standards in the world. They come because they have faith in us."

"Is that what happened a few moments ago? You call that faith? Is that what you call standards?"

"There are problems everywhere around the world; there are problems within every system. But we should not leave millions of suffering people in a country of billions and go ahead to serve where things are easier. What will happen to the people here then? Will they go abroad to treat themselves? People who do not even have enough resources to feed themselves properly, do you expect them to afford a medical treatment outside the country?"

"You can stay here with your ideals. Nobody really stops you."

"But the way you think is nowhere close to a doctor should think."

"Oh, well…yes. I have my own thinking, ideals and priorities. Who are you to tell me otherwise?"

Realizing the conversation was going to heat up, soon Subhash interfered, "Let's leave it. Things are solved now, right? Thanks to Sunil. He made the patients understand the truth. Now let's go. You are forgetting we have to attend a seminar down there," he gestured to the preparations going on below.

They headed downstairs to attend the seminar and at the same time the universe conspired to bring about a momentous transformation in Sunil's life.

⁘

College auditorium was crowded. Participants were preparing and performing on the cultural eve of college.

The campus was swarming with people. The four friends pushed their way through the crowd. The sun shone bright above the head and the temperature kept on soaring. The crowd reeked of a mixed odor of perfume and sweat. They managed their way to a clearing. There were not enough seats for everyone. The gallery was mostly filled up by young enthusiastic first year MBBS students.

Sunil and Rakesh also entered the auditorium.

Sunil and Subhash looked up and followed Rakesh's gaze as he looked towards the massive white screen put up on the makeshift platform ahead of them.

"Bhai, where is sister-in-law? On the screen?" mocked Subhash.

"Bhai, the projector hasn't even been turned on. Keep looking that way, she just walked in behind the screen. Any moment she will come out of the other side, like the moon comes out from behind the clouds…" and they all laughed out aloud.

Rakesh abruptly stopped laughing, "Look, look, there she comes…"

A golden yellow end of a *dupatta* emerged from behind the screen, they looked on. She came out along with three to four other girls. She had worn a simple brown and yellow cotton suit; her *dupatta* well pleated and folded ran down from her left shoulder. Her hair was tied up in a loose bun that rested low on the back of her shoulders. A few unruly strands of hair strayed out from here and there creating "perfect sinusoidal waves of lower amplitude and greater wavelength…"

⁂

"That was my definition though…" Rakesh laughed out loud along with Sam and Ajay. "But jokes apart,

Shalini was really someone nobody could miss even in a crowd of hundreds no matter however she tried to keep a low profile or dress so simply in the way she had that day."

"So, what happened next?" Sam asked excited.

She turned left, along with her friends and started walking towards them. "Sunil, she has to be our sister-in-law."

"Please stop talking rubbish. Let's go and stand near the gallery. If a group leaves, we can quickly get a seat there."

"You know nothing, Sunil. If a group leaves, we would offer the seats to the girl and her friends," Subhash remarked and winked at Rakesh.

Rakesh raised his palm in the air and Subhash slapped it with his own as they shared a laugh together. Sunil insisted them to stop. But they didn't.

"Look, Sunil. She is a perfect match for you. Just wait for her to look at you. She is coming in this direction and at any moment she might turn your eyes to you."

Sunil pushed them forward towards the gallery. As the four friends were going to turn Sunil stole a quick look at the girl, trying to hide it from his friends.

But Rakesh had noticed it already. "Keep looking, bhai. She will look at you."

No sooner had he finished his sentence than the girl grew alert sensing a pair of eyes stealing a look at her. She was trying her best to not look at that direction, but she turned her eyes finally at Sunil. Their eyes met. And it ended in a flash and both of them went their way; their gazes at the path ahead. A wish lingered somewhere deep down in Sunil's heart without him even knowing about it… the wish to read those lovely eyes.

Sunil had been going through a phase of tremendous pressure. The responsibility to look after 30 patients had been divided among the four doctors in his department. Even after working for sixteen to seventeen hours a day, it seemed not enough and he needed to stretch his hours. Due to this immense pressure many MD doctors leave the degree mid-way, being unable to cope with the stress. But Sunil was not one of them. He only knew to push himself further and further. One among the four in his department had left course and the responsibility of his patients came upon Sunil. He was now handling thirty patients a day. His seniors had even failed to notice that he was in such tremendous stress.

After lunch and a little afternoon nap he was up with his studies. This was a couple of days after the day of the seminar. Sunil's room was well lit and he never needed to switch on the electric lights during the day time. It was summer and there was much light even at 7 o' clock in the evening. Unlike the rest of India, in western states the sun set only at 7 in the evening or later in summer times. Sunil was busy studying and forgot to catch a glimpse of the beautiful sundown.

He heard a knock on the door. He knew it was Rakesh by the way of his knocking the door. He arose and proceeded to open the door, but Rakesh's patience was the most volatile thing on earth. The knock transformed into banging within seconds.

No sooner had Sunil opened the door than Rakesh held him by the arm and dragged him out, "Bhai Sunil, come I'll show you something today." He started walking through the corridor.

"Bhai Rakesh, what happened?"

Rakesh did not reply and dragged him to the staircase. Sunil wondered as they climbed up the steps.

"Go, Sunil. Tell me how it's looking from here?"

Sunil was silent for a moment. Many days and years have passed since he last came to stand on a roof top. He remembered his own roof in Muradpur...the etchings he had made in all its walls. Then life happened and responsibilities and pressure built up over his head and barred his vision so much so that he had long forgotten that an open sky existed above it.

"It's a beautiful view from here, Rakesh. It's been a long time that I have seen a pretty sunset like this. Thank you." He smiled cordially.

"Yes. The sunset is indeed very beautiful. Let the sun set first and I'll show you something that will make your view more beautiful."

"What is it?"

"Wait...you have to wait until the sun sets otherwise you won't be able to see properly."

"I will see properly when the sun sets? Bhai, if you want to abuse me say it to my face. Don't imply implicitly that I am an *ullu* (owl)."

"Talk less dear. Now you won't see it even after the sun sets. Look, there's power cut in the area ahead..." Rakesh said disheartened.

The sun had set. The two friends turned their back towards the crimson glow of the set sun and continued to talk.

Suddenly Rakesh turned around and screamed in joy, "Look Sunil, look there."

Sunil turned and followed Rakesh's pointed finger directed towards a white building not too far away from their building. He pointed particularly at a window. The whole area was under a power cut and many rooms were faintly aglow with candlelight. It was just like any other such rooms. The inside was faintly lit up and another candle rested on the window ledge. The quivering flame could be seen from afar.

"Have a look at that window. It's her room. I have managed to collect all possible information about her. Where she stays, with whom she stays, how many girls are there sharing her room, who is her best friend, phone number..."

"And you forgot only one thing in the long process. Her name."

"No, why would I? Shalini. It's Shalini."

"Shalini."

The name lingered on Sunil's tongue.

"Bhai Sunil, here, take her hostel's phone number and call her tonight. Come with me right now to our hostel's phone."

"Have you gone nuts? What would I say and what would she think? I am not going anywhere." There was an apprehensive panic on Sunil's face.

"Yes, you are going. Nothing will happen and she will concede, I am sure. I have seen love in her eyes for you dear…" Rakesh said in a poetic style.

Sunil was half convinced and half hopeful. He decided to take the chance.

The Phone room was occupied. Sunil and Rakesh waited outside fidgeting. After the phone was vacated, he waited for a moment gathering his courage and with a little boost from Rakesh he went inside and dialed the number.

The caretaker of the girl's hostel picked up the phone.

"Hello, I am Dr. Sunil. Can I talk to Dr. Shalini?"

"Please hold on," the caretaker had left to call Shalini. Any moment, she would pick up the phone.

Sunil's heartbeat quickened. He had come here to study the heart but he never knew that a day would come when his own heart will be out of his control. He imagined a variety of probable conversations in his mind, and how would he reply to them. But the reality is seldom similar to what people imagine.

"Hello?" a fine voice came from the other side of the connection. Sunil was so absorbed and tensed that he did not respond.

"Hello? Who's there?" repeated the voice. Sunil realized if he would say nothing then she will put the phone down.

"Hello…Hi, I am Dr. Sunil…"

"Yes. Tell me…"

"Uhh… I had asked to call…um…called to ask that if you would like to go for a coffee with me?"

His heart pounded in his chest as he waited for the answer. After few seconds the line became dead and a beep sounded recurrently. She had cut the line.

Rakesh was waiting outside all this time, impatiently. Sunil came out of the booth hanging his face down.

"What happened?" Rakesh asked.

"She cut the line…" Sunil said sullenly. Then suddenly he started to shout at Rakesh, "I should have never yielded to your "brilliant" ideas. Now think what she would think of me, she would tell her friends. What will be my reputation in the Girl's hostel?"

Sunil went off in a sulking mood.

"I know Sunil that she will ultimately come to like you," said Rakesh, helplessly watching him go away.

After that day Sunil often found Shalini on his way. Sometimes in the corridors he would find her walking towards him from the opposite direction… a lurking hope would ignite in his mind. But Shalini would completely ignore him and go away past him.

Few days later he unintentionally came into her way in the library. Seeing him walking through a furrow between book stacks Shalini would move away to another furrow. Sunil could realize everything and it pained him to see what had become of what he had expected. They both picked up their choice of books and submitted it to the librarian. The librarian asked both to fill the borrowing card inserted in a pocket at the back leaf of the books. Shalini searched for a pen while Sunil had started to fill up. There would always be a single pen tied with a string that would hang from the librarian's desk. Everybody used that pen to fill up the borrowing card. The pen was now in Sunil's hand. Shalini saw that and started to search for her own pen in her bag. He saw her too and stopped. He offered the pen to her, but she totally ignored him as if he didn't even exist. He then put the pen down on the desk for her to take it from there. But she went away to the entry catalogue and took a pen from there to fill it up. Sunil waited for her to complete the process with the librarian first and after she left he continued his own procedures of borrowing the book.

Like this, they met several times afterwards in the laboratory or at the ground, but each time Shalini ignored him and gave an impression of looking through him as if he didn't exist at all.

Sunil was slowly realizing that he may have achieved much in his life but there existed few things that can't be achieved by his own persistence or merit. Still, he retained some hope in his mind until the day Rakesh unintentionally put a final nail on the coffin of his hopes.

The four friends were in the mess for lunch. It was their regular place for lunch and tea. The place would mostly be filled up with boys. Girls seldom went there. They usually preferred the in-house canteen which was more hygienic. Suddenly Shalini entered with three of her friends. Sunil's heart started pounding again. Food went down his gullet with much effort. He hoped that she might have come there to see Sunil. Nobody knew it might truly have been the reason of her coming unless Rakesh would have done a great mistake unintentionally. He crooned in a severely out of tune voice,

"Abhi na jaao chood kar..."

Shalini instantly left along with her friends, disappointment clearly showing on her face as it grew red with humiliation and disgrace. Rakesh got a good verbal beating from the more sensible Subhash and Abhishek. Sunil was in no mood for any discussion on the topic henceforth. He had given up entirely and believed that he had other better things to do. He had a very critical patient under his care for whom he worked under a senior cardiologist.

Rakesh and Subhash were planning how to reach Shalini, through her father or friend or both but everything failed.

⁂

Sunil was working in the medical ward, doing his routine duty. It was already late in the evening. All other doctors in general shifts had either left or were preparing to leave. The night shifters had started to come in. At this moment nursing staff came in. The staff informed him that the patient in Critical Care Unit bed no. 6, is in very critical condition and senior resident Dr. Sandeep had asked him to immediately report in the CCU.

He rushed to the critical care unit and saw Dr. Sandeep struggling to keep the life breath stay in his body. Dr. Sandeep instructed Sunil to perform chest massage on the patient. Patient was suffering from acute heart attack with severe bradycardia. This was the first time that Sunil was experiencing such a situation where he realized how important the heart was. A little mistake on the part of any one present there, from senior resident Dr. Sandeep to MD student himself, would cause the worst thing to happen. He realized that one day would come when he will be standing along with Dr. Sandeep. He needed to learn and practice very well without letting his attention divert anywhere else. He had made up his mind when the situation was slowly going out of his control.

He looked at Dr. Sandeep once. He nodded, assuring him. Sunil took a deep breath, relaxed and started to perform CPR on the patient. This is one of the last steps, which is in the hands of a doctor to save his patient in case of cardiac arrest. If this fails, the doctor fails to save his patient. With the patient's BP falling severely, Dr. Sandeep decided to shift the patient to Cathlab to put TPI (Temporary Pacemaker Implantation) from ICU, as soon as possible. Sunil continued performing CPR on the patient all along while he was being moved from the ICU to the elevator, to the Cathlab in the stretcher. Sunil was on his highest sense of consciousness as he was aware that he was performing CPR on a moving patient. He had never in his life seen, experienced or heard about a situation like this. But his hands didn't tremble, his spirit and ability to work under pressure made him more efficient than he could be in a little easier situation.

It is said that we don't use even five percent of our brain in normal condition. But that day, that moment Sunil literally gave more than his hundred percent. After a few minutes of tensed efforts, the flat lines on the cardiac monitor started to peak and drop. Dr. Sandeep patted Sunil on the back. He wiped the sweat off his forehead and shook hands with his senior. Today he knew how much more important his field of specialization was in comparison to several others.

Sunil was on a regular walk to his patients' wards. Rakesh accompanied him. They came together into the ward of the patient whose life he had saved yesterday. The patient's wife sat beside the bed. As they came on a round, she did not greet them and kept on looking at Sunil with angry eyes. Sunil tried to ignore it at first and asked the patient after his health and how he felt at present. But at the back of his mind, he felt growingly uncomfortable by the way the woman's eyes were fixed on him.

He quickly completed his round and exited the ward. The woman silently followed behind and halted at the door. She lurched forward and peeked at Sunil until he traversed the whole corridor and descended onto the staircase which was not visible from where the woman was standing. As he vanished from her sight the woman followed him till downstairs but keeping enough distance between herself and him so as to not let Sunil be aware of her presence.

Sunil crossed the lift lobby and stepped onto the waiting room for patients' relatives. The woman followed. Sunil crossed the reception area and was about to pull open the exit door when the woman came from behind him and held him by the arm to turn him around. Sunil was in a perplexed state. He could not understand what was going on.

"Who are you?" demanded the woman.Sunil did not speak. He was utterly bewildered at the question thrown at his face by the elderly woman.

"I repeat, who are you? Who do you think you are?" The voice of the woman came across as authoritative.

The people sitting in the waiting room turned towards them. They expected a brawl to break out soon. They were almost sure that this doctor had done something wrong, like killed a patient may be…Now he is going to get a good beating from the patient's family.

Sunil remained dumbfounded.

"Our children are settled abroad. They are least bothered about what is happening here in India, their home. They are happily passing their days in tranquility and luxury of the amenities available there. They haven't come to visit their dying father whom you saved. Then why do you care so much? Why do you forget your sleep, food, off days and work tirelessly to save people you don't know? Who are we to you?" The woman shook him and tears rolled down her wrinkled cheeks.

There was a pin drop silence in the waiting hall. Shalini was present there, talking with a patient's relative. Rakesh had come following them both. Everybody's attention was on Sunil and the woman.

"Come sit here, please…" the woman took him by the arm and seated him on a chair and sat down beside him.

Sunil, like a hypnotized man, followed her and did as she said. The woman reached inside her satchel and took out a little lunch box. She opened it, tore a piece of *methiparantha* and fed it to him.

"I saw you come to my husband's ward every day. I saw you spend morning to evening at duty. I knew you stayed without lunch several days a week. You killed your hunger by drinking multiple cups of coffee. You take care everyone but yourself. There should be someone to take care of you. If you fall sick, who will come to the rescue of people like us?" she continued as she put pieces of *parantha* into his mouth one after other. "The girl who will marry you will be indeed a lucky girl. God bless you, child…"

Rakesh was happily watching the scene. He knew his friend deserved to see a day like this that seldom doctors ever see in their lives. Suddenly he noticed Shalini standing in a corner, her eyes fixed on Sunil and a gleaming smile slowly spreading on her lips giving a peachy glow to her cheeks. Rakesh smiled in his mind. The thing which he had tried to do from a long time was finally done by this old woman.

✦

Rakesh and Sunil's many of his other friends had come to appreciate him on account of the events that had happened a few days ago. It was one of those days in the hospital when the crowd of patients and relatives was much less. Abhishek and Subhash were having an off day, but they were missing from the morning. Sunil and Rakesh sat at the lobby sipping a cup of coffee.

It was late afternoon and a long slanting beam of sunlight came in through the entrance of the lobby. Sunil did not notice when two elongated shadows appeared on the beam of sunlight. The two shadows approached Sunil. Rakesh turned his face towards them and his jaws dropped. Sunil, following Rakesh's unusual expression turned to the shadows.

Shalini stood there with Suman, her best friend.

"Congratulations, Dr. Sunil. I saw what had happened that day. It is one of the greatest experiences a doctor can be fortunate enough to have in his whole life. You made us all proud. Meet my friend Suman, she is the one who suggested that a doctor like you should be celebrate," she said with a little hesitation in her voice.

"Thank you so much," Sunil replied with a smile.

The two women turned and started to walk towards the door. Sunil kept looking on.

Rakesh almost shouted, "I said... I told you..."

Sunil kept looking at the long retreating shadows. Suddenly the shadow seemed to change shape in a peculiar manner. Sunil's eyes shot up.

Abhishek, Subhash, few other doctors and assistants entered the lobby hauling a stretcher. Their faces were pale like death. They rushed the stretcher into the lab and the door of the lab slammed close. Sunil and Rakesh ran up to the door. They watched through the little glass opening. The man on the stretcher was one of their colleagues, a doctor himself. He turned and twisted and threw his limbs in agitation and pain. Abhishek and Subhash came out, leaving him under the care of one of the best senior doctors in the college and his assistants.

"He is from the chest and TB department. He caught tuberculosis meningitis and is very critical." They moved away from the door and waited on a bench kept by the wall of the corridor. After a few moments the door creaked and everyone stood up in alertness and anxiety.

"He is dead," stated the senior doctor leaving all of them utterly dumbstruck. They couldn't comprehend the horror of the situation at once. They could not believe that one of their colleagues was gone, treating people.

Abhishek stormed at Sunil. "I hope now you have realized what I tried to put across that day. The reward for treating people of this country is right in front of your eyes. His parents had sent him to study MD in the hope that someday he will help his family and save lives. And now very soon they will rush in to take out his corpse from the hospital morgue. There are no amenities for the doctors who work in such unhygienic conditions to protect themselves. And there is no effort from part of the authorities to improve the unhygienic conditions. They don't care for the lives of the men who are the lifesavers. Now decide for yourselves if there's any wrong in what I say."

Sunil silently listened. He knew Abhishek's arguments were right. He had nothing to say today. The death of this young doctor raised many questions in his head. He needed an answer to them all. He stealthily sneaked out of the crowded corridor and headed for the lake side he would visit often, Pichola Lake. It gave him the tranquility of mind that was required to think and reason properly.

He came out of the hospital into the fresh air of the grounds. It was not any ornamental lake. It was not adorned by well-maintained flowering plants or anything. Wild bushes, cactus and large trees had grown around it. As he neared the lake the smell of damp earth sensitized him. His nostrils had become numbed by the mixed smell of Dettol, blood, urine and strong phenyl in the hospital. The fresh air clarified his mind and he quietly sat down on the lake side. Suddenly he heard Rakesh's voice from far away behind. He turned and saw Rakesh sprinting towards him decelerating his speed as he came closer.

"When did you slip out from amongst us?" asked Rakesh.

"Sit down, Rakesh," Sunil said softly.

As Rakesh sat down Sunil again asked him, "Tell me one thing, Rakesh. Is our medical system really that bad, like what Abhishek thinks? Hundreds and thousands of patients are treated by a doctor in his lifetime without the system providing anything for their safety and protection. Isn't it unfair? May be, Abhishek was right. Our efforts are really rewarded in the west, not here. Maybe I had become too idealistic... But if all the doctors leave the country to treat people elsewhere just because they are protected and rewarded there properly, who would treat the penniless and helpless masses of India?"

"Sunil, you are thinking too much at this moment. Keep these thoughts aside for some times and focus on your personal life a bit. Shalini had come to you to congratulate. I suggest you should call her once." Rakesh prompted Sunil.

"And what if she again cuts the line?" asked Sunil half convinced.

"She won't. Trust me, this time she won't," Rakesh put a hand on Sunil's shoulder.

⁂

The late afternoon was slowly yielding away to dusk. The electric lights on the roads inside their campus lit up one by one. The telephone room was empty as if time had been waiting for Sunil. It was just the perfect time. Sunil went inside, closed the door and reluctantly dialed the number. Rakesh waited outside.

"Hello?" the voice sounded from the other side.

"Hello, this is Dr. Sunil. May I speak to Dr. Shalini?"

"Please hold on…" the voice trailed off.

This time Sunil was perfectly at peace with himself. His heart maintained its normal pace. Perfect calmness and composure reflected on his face.

"Hello, is it Dr. Sunil?"

"Yes…"

"Tell me doctor saab," and Sunil could hear the smile that spread on her lips as she said the word 'doctor saab', making her look prettier.

"Can I take you for coffee?" Sunil asked and a silence prevailed for a few moments on both the sides.

⁂

Rakesh was pacing up and down outside the booth when Sunil came out with a blank look in his eyes hanging his head, exactly the way he came out of this booth the last time he had called Shalini.

"What happened? Did she cut the line again?"

"No. She agreed to go with me."

"See? I had told you. You never believed in me. I can read minds, you see it now. I told you, I told you." He jumped in exhilaration and hugged Sunil patting him loudly on his back.

Sunil smiled and the two friends walked away to their quarters.

Rakesh was sitting alone in their mess sipping a cup of tea unmindfully. Abhishek and Subhash joined him. This was the place where the four friends had their evening tea every day.

"Where's Sunil?" asked Subhash

"He is on off-day." Rakesh replied with a mischievous glint in his eyes.

"Did he take an off from breakfast too?" mocked Abhishek.

"Absolutely not, he will spend his evening, not with us but someone else."

"With whom?" Subhash and Abhishek asked in chorus.

"Shalini…" Rakesh replied as an impish smile played on his lips.

"What? Seriously?" Subhash almost screamed.

"He just went out with his bike. He is waiting down at the parking lot."

⁂

Shalini had silently arrived behind Sunil while he was waiting. The three friends watched from a distance and laughed.

Today Shalini had stopped trying to look simplistic. Her cotton suit had been replaced by a nude pink georgette suit with little black embroidery. Her hair was flowing open. Sunil noticed for the first time that Shalini had waist long hair like dark waves. Some of the hair strands played over her face with the mild breeze of the morning. Sunil's heart urged to push those hair strands behind her ears. But he kept himself from doing it with much difficulty.

"Good evening," Shalini greeted Sunil as he was too taken to speak.

"Good evening," he replied nervously.

As Sunil started the bike, Shalini moved behind him to sit. A smile played on the lips of both unseen to each other.

As the bike drove away Rakesh felt a tranquil happiness for his friend. He knew he deserved it. My friend, your life is finally settled… so happy for you, he smiled within.

⚜

Sunil returned from his date with Shalini late in the evening. He was just about to put his key into the keyhole when Rakesh jumped up before him from nowhere.

"So, how was it?"

Sunil blushed like a teenage boy, "Come in."

"So, when is your next meeting?" Rakesh jabbed Sunil in the ribs.

"I don't know. I will call her tomorrow evening and set it up."

"Oh, well… What is my reward for setting you up?"

"What do you want? Just tell me."

"Today evening when you call her, I will be there inside the booth." Rakesh winked impishly.

⚜

Sunil and Rakesh reached the telephone room late in the evening. The surroundings were quieter. As Sunil dialed the number Rakesh could clearly hear the ring.

"Bhai Sunil… Say something new to her. You have asked her out for coffee twice already."

Sunil nodded but couldn't manage to think up of anything new to speak to Shalini. "Tell me, Dr. saab," Shalini spoke up instead of saying 'Hello', as she knew it was none other than Sunil.

"How are you Shalini?"

"I am good, Dr. saab. Now tell me why you called me, without beating around the bush."

Rakesh wanted to laugh out loud at Shalini's humor but checked himself fearing that he might annoy her if she senses any other person's presence. He simply covered his mouth with his palms and clenched his fists to keep himself from laughing.

"Let's go for coffee tomorrow evening?"

"We already had coffee."

"But that was cold drink. Let's go for coffee."

Shalini's laughter sounded like tinkling bells from the other side of the connection. And Sunil understood, it was a yes.

Shalini took consent from her parents and started meeting frequently. Dr. Sunil completed his MD and left for Delhi where he did his senior residency and prepared for MD entrance test and both got married.

⁂

"What happened next?" Sam asked with his eyes gleaming with the curiosity to know further.

"Sorry, Mr. Sam. My journey with Sunil was till this point in his life and it ends here. If you want to know further about his life and struggles you must go and meet Shalini, his wife. She has been his constant companion from then onwards. I can tell that you will definitely go there. So, take the contact number of Shalini." Rakesh searched the contact list of his phone and wrote it down on a piece of paper."Thank you so much, Rakesh, for your time." Sam extended his hands for a handshake.

"Best wishes for your book that you are going to create about the story of this great man," Rakesh held Sam's hand and spoke.

⁂

Dusk had already started to creep in. Clouds accumulated on the southern corner of the sky. Ajay feared that they would have to face another heavy spell of rain just like the previous day. He held open the car door to Sam.

"Should we speak to Dr. Shalini first, or should we head straight to her house?"

"Sam, I know you are too excited. But look at the sky. This is no village or Muradpur. This is Jaipur. If a heavy spell of rain starts now, we would be totally stuck. There will be traffic jams all over the city. Also, it is going to be rush hours shortly. We must quickly return to our hotel. You haven't had a good meal or a good sleep from the last twenty-four hours. So, let's just retreat and relax today. We shall call Dr. Shalini tomorrow early morning. She too is a doctor. She must be busy. I think it would best to take an appointment first. What do you say?"

"Yes, you are right. Let's do as you suggest…" Sam shut the door of the back seat of the car and the car drove off.

FOUR

GOD'S PLAN

The top floor suite of the hotel elaborated a view of the dazzling city being washed by torrential shower, through its massive windowpanes that extended from the floor base to the ceiling. Thunder cracked across the dark skies and lighted up the bedroom for a moment. The lights in the room had not been put on. Sam threw himself down onto the bed and lighted a cigarette. His hands reached out to the phone and he started fidgeting with it. The light from the phone threw a blurry blue haze on the ceiling. He was planning to call Shalini when his phone started to buzz. It was Dr. Abhishek. Sam picked up the call.

"Hello, Dr. Abhishek, how are you?"

"I am fine, Sam. I hope you too are well. I was just wondering how your trip to India has been up until now, and how far you have proceeded in your work."

"To tell you the truth Dr. Abhishek, I would like to express my immense gratitude to you for advising me to write about Dr. Sunil. Not only have I found many truly inspiring stories but I have also found a love story here. And it is truly helping me build my story."

"Yes, I've heard that you are all set to meet Shalini. I had a few words with her regarding this. She will be meeting you tomorrow. You should call her to finalize the timing."

"Yes sure, will do that. I also wish to meet Dr. Sunil once, the man I am writing my story about."

"That will be great. Please do write something about how brilliant doctors like Sunil need to serve in the right countries that deserve him, instead of being stuck in India. If a brilliant and famous author like you expresses his own thoughts and reflection on an issue, it instantly becomes a standard to follow."

"But Dr. Abhishek, as far as I have known this country and the inspiring life story of Sunil, I feel that his country needs him more than any other. If doctors like him leave to serve others what will become of the ailing and the diseased who are too poor to afford a pricey treatment?"

"Hmm…however, did you speak to Shalini yet?"

"No, Ajay will let me know."

"Okay… All the best. Goodnight."

"Goodnight," Sam put the phone down on the bedside table.

There was a knock on the door. Sam knew it was Ajay. He had come to let him know about the appointment timings with Shalini.

"Sharp at 9 tomorrow morning," Ajay peeped without entering the room as Sam opened the door. Sam set the alarm and went off to sleep after Ajay left.

⁂

Sam and Ajay sat in the expansive dining hall on the first floor. It was early in the morning and the hall was almost empty and quiet except a few hotel staffs moving around and a couple of other guests. The surroundings prevailed in the silence of early morning except a television buzzing in the lowest volume. Ajay was gorging onto a sandwich and casually going through the first page of the day's newspaper.

Sam suddenly called out to him, "Ajay, just look once. Isn't that Dr. Sunil's hospital?"

Ajay looked at the television screen. The top news channel of the region was airing the disturbing news of an angry mob in a demolishing rage gathered in front of a hospital gate. They shouted and hurled stones at the building and its gates. There was rage and complaints in the voices of people as they condemned the doctors and hospital for the death of a young woman.

"No, it isn't Sunil's hospital. It's some other in the city," Ajay replied.

After almost a minute of silence Sam replied hesitantly, "I have another thought right now."

"What is it?" Ajay asked.

"In a place where there is so much hatred and mistrust among people regarding the honesty and competency of doctors… I don't know… but I feel the book I am going to write may backfire."

"Relax Sam… these are one in a million cases around the country. It happens sometimes. You need not worry."

"I am still doubtful. I don't want to scar my reputation after all."

"You are thinking too much, Sam. Let's finish our breakfast quickly; our appointment with Dr. Shalini is within half an hour."

Shalini sat in her cabin fiddling with a paper weight on her table. She managed to reach the hospital a little earlier this morning since her daughters' school had declared leave on the rainy day due to the water logging within the city. She waited for Mr. Sam and Ajay.

There was a knock on her door and after her vocal approval from within, it was pushed open by a staff who informed her about the arrival of her intended guests. She asked him to bring them inside.

As the two men followed the staff Shalini looked up and smiled back at Ajay who was already smiling at her. But to her surprise, she found Sam a little disturbed.

As the staff left closing the door behind him, Shalini asked Sam with her doctor's instinct, "Anything wrong, Mr. Sam?"

"Yes. If you don't mind, I would like to ask you something."

"Please…"

"While coming inside we noticed a few policemen in uniform…standing near the entrance. Is everything alright?"

"It's absolutely alright. They do come sometimes. On the occasions of emergency cases of accidents or even family members becoming ill… they keep coming. So, tell me what you want to know about Sunil."

Ajay spoke first to Shalini's question, "Sam has come to know a detailed account of Sunil's life while he pursued his DM in cardiology, the struggles he faced and how he recovered."

Shalini looked out of the window and recounted the time when Sunil went to take the entrance exam of SGPGI. He cleared the exam and got selected.

"He was very lucky to have got his *Dronacharya* in his HOD Dr. Nakul Sinha at SGPGI Lucknow. He was like the commander general who lead his battalion of soldiers efficiently and skillfully," Shalini said.

✦

Sunil sat with fellow doctors inside the auditorium. He looked around. Many seats were empty. This was induction of higher qualification degrees like DM. Not many doctors have the thirst for knowledge and ambition to go continuously up the ladders of medical studies. But Sunil always had it in him. He sat eagerly waiting for the program to start, his eyes beaming with excitement.

Suddenly a tall shadow fell on the screen. Someone had come in front of the projector. He is Dr. Nakul Sinha, HOD. Sunil watched.

"Dear doctors, you are already so much accomplished in life that you could really have started practicing privately and independently. You are like the bamboo that takes years to sprout from the soil but once it does, it grows quickly to reach the top. Likewise, you will be quick to reach the knowledge of all elements. So, never forget to always show the way towards light to others and inspire, to always remain a bamboo in the lives of the people around you."

Shalini was hurrying in the kitchen. A little glass bowl fell to the ground and shattered. "Sunil, nothing will remain intact in this kitchen if you hurry me up every day like this. This is the seventh item I broke."

"I will buy you fourteen more. I am getting late, Shalini. I will have something from the canteen."

"Wait. If you don't have time to have your breakfast I will pack it for you. You can't have food outside every day and maintain a good health."

Shalini packed it as he rushed out of his home and sat in the car. Shalini came running and threw it into the car through the window as the car started and swiftly drove off. Shalini stood there for a moment, thinking. From the day he had joined his DM this was a regular routine.

She felt it won't take much time before his health starts dwindling. She had to do something. Months passed in this way. The trees in their garden had shed their leaves and turned green once again.

Shalini had looked at the clock several times in the last one hour. This was the time Sunil generally returned home. But no one can tell for sure when a doctor would return home. Being a doctor herself, Shalini knew that and never tried to call him. She just waited eagerly and walked up and down unable to concentrate in anything. Anyone who would look at her would be deceived into thinking that she was in deep worry.

The bell rang at last. Shalini ran to open it. Sunil had returned. She took the coat and the chest from Sunil's hands. Sunil saw the glow that was spread on her face, making her look more beautiful. Sunil just kept looking at her. Putting all things in their own places Shalini ran down to him with a glass of water. She sat down beside him and held out the glass. Sunil took it from her hand but kept it down on the table.

"You want to say something. Tell me," Sunil asked.

Shalini blushed and rested her head on Sunil's shoulder putting her arms in his and releasing her weight upon him.

"You have become so heavy, dear…" Sunil teased Shalini.

Shalini quickly raised her head in mock anger and said, "Yes, I have and can't you think why? Don't you think I can be pregnant?"

Sunil stared into Shalini's eyes for a few moments and when he was convinced that her eyes told the truth he put his arms around her and hugged her tight.

"Sunil… You are stinking. First go and wash yourself," Shalini gently pushed him away and smiled.

Shalini was happy and she could realize how happy Sunil was from his every move and words. They both were very happy. But Shalini found out during the initial days of her pregnancy that Sunil had almost started to forget the news of her pregnancy. All he cared about was his work. It was as if he hadn't married Shalini but his work.

⚜

Like every other day Shalini had packed the lunch for Sunil. It was well past lunch time, but he hadn't found the time to have it yet. He was walking through the corridor towards his cabin. He felt tired to the bone. His muscles were aching and his palms were clammy. Drops of perspiration flowed down from the back of his head. He opened his cabin door and straightaway sat down on his chair. He drank some water and rested for a few moments. His head reeled. He knew he had still half a day of work and duty hours left and so took out a paracetamol from his drawer. He had just kept it down on the table to take some water when the cabin door handle turned without any knock and a nurse peeped in, "Sir, Dr. Goyal asked for you."

"Let's go," Sunil arose from the chair and followed the nurse.

There was a patient for whom Sunil did an eco-cardiogram and advised that biventricular pacing can be useful in that patient. Biventricular pacing was found useful in trial in a certain subset of heart failure patients and Dr. Goyal was planning his first biventricular pacing in that patient. He asked to assist him in his biventricular pacing implantation.

After the biventricular pacing Dr. Sunil was relieved and happy that he could identify a patient where new technology device is used in cardiology stream.

The procedure continued for four hours.

During the weekend, Dr. Nakul Sinha had arranged a dinner party at his place. All the department doctors were present there with their spouses. "Now tell me Sunil, what are your plans after you've done your DM?" asked Dr. Nakul.

"Sir, I am just concentrating on completing my DM right now. I don't want to get distracted by thinking about the future."

Shalini interrupted, "Sir, I had suggested him that he should move abroad. He will get to learn a lot more there. Their medical sciences and researches are far more advanced than ours. What do you think, Sir? Make him realize if you think I am not wrong."

"Yes, you're right. I am sure there will be many more things to learn, even after doing your DM," said Dr. Nakul. "There are new researches going on abroad, US to be specific. Or you can even settle there for better opportunities well deserved by a doctor like you."

"Sir, if I ever go abroad then it will be solely to pursue studies or attend seminars or programs. I will never settle abroad."

"But Sunil, with your talent and dedication you deserve a better environment and workplace to nurture your skill."

"I too feel like that, Sir. It's only you who can make him understand what he should do," Shalini said.

"Shalini is right, Sunil. You should consider once on this matter. Take your time and then decide. Just don't be too emotional."

"No, Sir. I have long made up my mind. I was born to serve my nation."

✦

Sunil was so adamant about pursuing his career in his own country that sometimes it even disappointed Shalini. Sunil was driving back home. Shalini was disturbed. She quietly sat beside him and kept looking outwards without once turning her face to him. Few heated questions of Shalini were answered indifferently by Sunil during this time. She felt exasperated by the extent and depth of his determination to not leave his country to settle abroad.

✦

The morning sun rays peeped in through the slit between two curtains. The alarm had started to buzz. Sunil quickly half raised his head from the pillow and stopped the buzz, then looked at Shalini sleeping soundly by him. He was careful not to wake her up since she had been six months pregnant and needed good rest. He looked at her serene face and planted the lightest kiss on her forehead before sliding down the bed.

Shalini was up by the time Sunil came in with breakfast. She looked at him for few moments and cherished the care that he showered on her.

"It's all too much, Sunil. I will put on weight…and it's already showing." Shalini made a baby face expressing her false concern.

Being a doctor, she knew it was part of the process. She yearned to see time and again how Sunil cared for her; how he doted on her. Few words of tenderness would melt her each time.

"Take this," Sunil handed a chit of paper to Shalini, "These are emergency numbers of the hospital; I may not carry my phone all the time as you already know, but do call me at any moment in these numbers. I will be there for you at once."

"Sure, Doctor saab. But you do know that you are a cardiologist and not a gynecologist, don't you?" Shalini said with a pinch of humor.

Sunil silently continued to prepare the basic instruction for Shalini and himself. She watched him with unwavering eyes. Suddenly she realized how caring this man could be when it came to her and their child. But every moment of thankfulness for having something was always paired with a fear of losing it. "Sunil, you will never forget us, right?" She asked with a wistful look in her eyes.

"Dear, I can never forget you even if I go into comatose. And if I ever recover from that state, you will be the first one I will remember."

"How will you remember me then… gradually or rapidly?" jokingly asked Shalini.

"Neither gradually, nor rapidly; Instantly." Sunil smiled at her. His smile assured her from deep within.

⁂

The day had been tiring. Sunil had skipped lunch as usual as many other days. He leaned back in his chair. The door of his cabin was closed. For the first time out of tiredness he wished for no more visitors or staffs calling him to attend a patient. He was bone weary. He longed to go home, he longed for a touch of comfort from his dear, loving Shalini, to rest his aching head on her lap. He looked at the clock. It was 8 PM already. He came out of his cabin once and looked both sides along the corridor. It was deserted. The regular staff had also left. He felt a little dizzy. He closed the door back and approached the wash basin in his cabin. He splashed some water on his face and took up his white coat and rested it on his arms. Taking the keys from his table he locked the cabin from outside as he left. But he remembered he should have something to eat before he started for his home. So, he took the way towards the cafeteria.

There were few doctors in the night duty all of whom had assembled there to have their dinner.

Someone asked Sunil, "Hey Sunil, Ritesh told me he saw you in the morning shift. And you're still working?

"No, actually I am just leaving," smiled back Sunil.

"Whatever man, it means you were working until now. Take care man…you are over working without a doubt."

Sunil didn't reply but responded with a smile. But someone called him again, "Sunil, you look exhausted. Is everything alright?"

Sunil stared at him blankly for a few moments and then replied, "Oh! Did we discharge that another patient?"

The two other doctors looked at each other, wondering how much related an answer they had received to the question that was asked. One of them spoke again to make sure their doubts were clear, "Hey, Sunil…are you sure you are fine?"

"Yes. I am fine. Why?" Sunil answered as if asked entirely out of the blue.

"Nothing, you just looked tired. That's why I asked." Smiled the other doctor as Sunil waved at him.

They did not press him further and let him go. Sunil felt the hunger dying away and did not wish any longer to have something. He pulled the car door, threw his white coat inside and then slumped down on the steering seat. He held the steering for a few moments and then heaving a sigh he turned the keys.

✕～ᏂᎾᎾᏂ～✕

Shalini stood still looking at the wall of their sitting hall, her both hands on her hips. She looked at it carefully, sometimes tilting her head this side and that side. The left end needs to go up a little bit, she murmured to herself and adjusted accordingly.

"Perfect," she said to herself.

A glow spread on her face. She turned round to see whether everything was perfect. The southeast, east, the northeast, the north and the northwest, the west and the southwest, every corner of the room was perfectly decorated with balloons, ribbons, lights and candles. She turned round again to face the wall to the south she was watching for so long. With pretty, colored balloons the beautifully decorated wall read 'HAPPY ANNIVERSARY'. Everything looked so perfect. She just needed one more thing, to utterly surprise Sunil. It was their first anniversary, she knew that. But she needed to do something that would really make him the happiest. She ran to the phone and started calling up Lallan, Sunil's best friend here, inviting him over to her place for dinner.

"Hello, Lallan?"

"Yes, is that Shalini?"

"Yes, Lallan. How are you?"

"Absolutely great Shalini, except for these extra hours of night duty…" Lallan laughed at his own joke.

"Oh, you are on night duty today?" Shalini's voice lacked the excitement.

"Yes, but why? Is there any problem?"

"No, Everything is fine. It's just our…anniversary… So I just thought—" Shalini couldn't finish the sentence when the bell rang. Shalini knew it was none other than Sunil. "Lallan, I think Sunil is back. Please try once to come over, even if it is a little late in the night. It would cheer up us both to have your company."

"I will try for sure."

Shalini hung up and went to open the door. She could not run but still hurried knowing that Sunil might be stressed and was becoming impatient having to wait so long. But she knew in her mind this was not the Sunil she knew for so many years. He never rang the bell more than twice. He had the keys. If it would ever take longer than usual, he would use the keys. However, Shalini overlooked everything in the joyous moment of this day.

She opened the door with a broad inviting smile on her face. Sunil stood outside, his coat hanging from his arms, his head tilted to one side, droplets of sweat rolling down his head and neck into darker patches in his shirt. He came inside walking slowly and looked around at all the decorations all around the house with incredulity.

"What are all these for?"

"Don't you remember today's date?" Shalini asked, a little hurt.

"20th Feb 2007. So? Why decorate the room so much?" Sunil asked surprised, clearly not getting anything.

"Don't you remember anything?" Shalini asked.

"Arre, what should I remember now? I have to prepare for DM entrance exam also. I know what you are talking about, that I have to speak to baba about you. I will speak at home about us only after DM entrance, otherwise my preparations will be disturbed." After a little pause and scrutinizing Shalini for a moment he spoke again, "And what are you doing in my house? Baba is posted here around Udaipur nowadays. If he sees us, everything will be ruined. And what are you doing in my room before marriage?"

He then pushes aside a confused Shalini and quickly enters and sits down on the sofa holding his head. "I have a headache, give me meds." Before Shalini could even react he again spoke, "I feel like vomiting now. Do one thing, give me pantaprozole."

Shalini goes into the kitchen without a word and came out holding a glass of water in her hand. As she bent forward to put the glass on the table in front of Sunil, her open hair fell off from her shoulders and dangled by the sides of her neck.

Sunil kept looking at her for some time and said, "You are looking so beautiful today. Is there anything special today that you have dolled up so much?"

"You seem too tired. Take rest," said Shalini handing him the glass of water. "So, you really don't remember anything about today?"

"We met today for the first time, right?" Sunil tried to guess.

"Who am I?" asked Shalini.

"You are Shalu. I have spoken to maa about us. But let me speak to baba once, then we will get married, for sure. I promise, my darling. By the way where are my books? Why did you put it inside? I have to prepare for my DM entrance," he continued in a daze, "Why is it stinking so much? May be from hostel kitchen… come let's go outside."

Just as he tried to get up, he sits down on the ground holding his head. Shalini rushed towards their bedroom to bring a pillow.

"Hey wait…stop. Why are you going inside my bedroom?" demanded Sunil.

"You've gone mad, Sunil… Do you even have any idea what rubbish you are saying?"

"Absolutely yes, I do. Who are you to enter my bedroom without my permission?"

"I am your wife, Sunil." Shalini clasped Sunil's shoulders and shook him.

Sunil vehemently freed himself from her clasp and retorted on to her face, "Behave yourself, please. I am sorry. I don't know you."

Shalini again moved forward and grabbed him by the shoulder. She shook him and he shouted harsher and louder. He tore off the decorations from here and there. She tried to calm him, she couldn't figure out what to do and what not to. He then knelt down on the floor pressing his head with both his hands.

Shalini carefully went near him and lifted him from the floor and seated him on the bed. "I want to go home," he said drooping his head down.

Shalini was just about to say that he *was* at home but then checked herself saying, "Yes, dear…We will go home. Get up, come with me."

By this time Shalini was sure that something had seriously happened to Sunil. She drove him off to the hospital.

⁂

Shalini took Sunil to the cardiology dept where Dr. Garg was still working late in the night. "What has happened Shalini? Why are you both at the hospital at this hour of the night?" "Sir, something really serious has happened to him. I don't know but he is speaking incoherent, meaningless things. He is having problem in recognizing people. Please do something, Sir. I am much worried."

"I see. Let me see. Bring him inside."

Doctor Garg examined him. After five to ten minutes of initial checkup he too looked tensed. Shalini was about to ask something but he dismissed her and started to call Dr. Nakul, the HOD.

"Sir, I am worried to inform you that Sunil has arrived in the hospital accompanied by his wife with altered sensorium and irreverent talk. Not really sure what has happened."

All this while, Shalini stood helpless waiting for Dr. Garg to speak to her.

"What did Dr. Nakul Sir say?" asked Shalini.

"Dr. Nakul asked for MRI and also said that 'He is our boy and we will treat him in our ICU'. He called neurologists to immediately start basic investigations and treatment."

Afterwards they took Sunil to the MRI. Lallan saw Shalini in the corridor.

"What has happened Shalini? Just hours back you were inviting me over, for your anniversary."

"I don't know anything, Sir. Please help me. I can't keep my calm anymore after what I've seen."

They admitted Sunil in ICU and sent him for the MRI. Lallan consulted radiologist doctor Gupta to instantly perform an MRI on Dr Sunil. Lallan moved out aside while the MRI scan was in progress and called Dr. Ritu to come and check Dr. Sunil as he was having neurological problem. Dr. Ritu was working as a senior resident in neurology. During the whole process everyone noticed the strangest Sunil they had ever known. He was a child. He placed his hands along the interior sides of the MRI scanner and fiddled with the machineries and suspended parts like someone who had seen something great for the first time.

"What is this new plaything you have installed here? No, no. Let me stay here for some time longer. I need to study it…" he fought with the staff as they struggled to take him out of the scanner.

Shalini exhaled and drooped down her shoulders. She felt like her feet drifting away. They shifted him to an ICU.

Suddenly she noticed a peculiar restlessness in him which was in addition to whatever she had witnessed so long. He looked like he had trouble in sitting still, leaning or drinking and everything else. He expressed non-cooperation in everything that was asked of him. He threw his arms and legs and his body shook at times. It was becoming increasingly difficult to create a channel through his wrist to collect blood samples. Sunil was fighting with the doctors and the doctors were struggling. Shalini could not watch any longer even after being a doctor herself.

The blood samples, MRI scan reports were all gone for examination. Sunil was put on ventilation as ordered by senior resident doctor. Shalini was lost in deep thought. Suddenly she remembered something she had heard a long time ago from someone she knew. Till today it was just some news but now it was so much more. She had once heard from Rakesh about a doctor in her MBBS college in Udaipur who died contracting disease from patients he was treating. She started to deduce and interpret meaningless outcomes from her thoughts. Suddenly her trance was broken by the voice of Dr. Sinha.

"How's Sunil now? Any updates?" he asked.

"Sir, he has been given a tranquilizer because he was growing restless. And…and…" hesitated Lallan.

"And what?" demanded Dr. Nakul Sinha.

"They are not able to reach any diagnosis so far, but it seems to be meningitis or encephalitis."

"Call the neurologist and after consulting, plan a lumber puncture. Not just ventilation. Put him on anything that is required. Do whatever that is necessary. Do everything. Save him, he is our boy."

Dr. Shalini couldn't speak anything. She started crying looking at the photo. After few minutes she asked Sahiram Ji to come to Lucknow as Sunil is not well.

✦

Dr. Lallan, Dr. Shalini and Dr. Ritu watched Sunil lying on hospital bed. It is already late in night 2 AM.

"Will Sunil be all right?" Shalini asked Dr. Lallan.

Dr. Lallan answered yes promptly but his face showed some worry. He said, "We will not leave any stone unturned to make Sunil alright. We have started antibiotic, antiviral and MRI. So, we will go for lumbar puncture in the morning."

✦

Sun's rays filtered in through the beaded strips of the curtains on each window along the corridor outside the ICU unit. Shalini still sat like a mound of immovable rock on the bench. She unmindfully watched from the corner of her eyes a pair of grey trousers approach her from her left. She heard the footsteps, too. But nothing registered in her head. Her trance broke with Lallan's voice, "Here, take this."Shalini looked up to find Lallan sipping a cup of tea and holding out another towards her.

"Reports?" She instantly asked the question the moment she saw Lallan. This was what she worried about the whole night.

"Nothing conclusive in the reports; I went through all of them myself."

"And these are the MRI scan reports. Nothing conclusive revealed in these either," Shalini heard Ritu's voice and turned.

"So, what do we do next?" asked Shalini to Ritu.

"Now we have planned for Lumbar puncture. Let's see if it reveals something. Did you notice any previous symptoms?" asked Ritu,

"Yes, he complained about vomits and headache regularly but he was working and managing with medicines."

"Hmm…" Ritu nodded.

⁂

Sunil was in half consciousness when his hands were freed and he was lying in a hunched stance, folding his knees. His spine made an arch when viewed from side.

Local anesthesia had been performed on his back. A point was marked on his back along the spine. A needle was pushed through that mark and his spinal fluid was collected. Sunil did not have much idea what was going on.

⁘

Her heart thumped in her chest as she wondered what she would encounter in the reports. She looked around here and there; she grazed the ceiling multiple times with her eyes. She felt like she was standing through an epoch in time.

"Here." Lallan came and held out the reports. Shalini's hands shook. She took it and opened it right there. Nothing conclusive. A list of tests revealed the same result. He too was confused after their last hope revealed no illness for which tests had been conducted.

"We have tried anti-bacterial and anti-viral but nothing is conclusive yet. Radiologist is also stressing upon that it is early stages of tuberculosis Meningitis," said Ritu. "So, we must start anti-tubercular drug."

"If we start anti-tubercular we have to continue it for 9 months. On the first we do not know what exactly has happened to him."

It was almost forty-eight hours that was spent in turmoil and confusions. Shalini did not know what was awaiting her in the future or what she should do. She desperately needed someone to put a hand on her shoulders to calm her down and just say that everything will be alright. But here she was, fighting Sunil's battle and her own, all alone. She never went home for a moment and constantly sat on that bench or walked outside Sunil's bed.

"Shalu beta," a voice melted her heart and it wanted to overflow. But she checked herself and turned around.

Sahiram stood at gates of the medical ICU, a jute bag hanging from his hands. Shalini rushed to him and took him inside and seated him on the chair. He held her hands and said, "Your mother has sent this for her child. I did not take her here because I didn't know how and in what condition I will have to see my Sunil. Take this and feed him, tell him that his ma has prepared this for him."

Shalini felt like her heart will burst out. She could not take it any longer.

"Baba," she clasped his hand with both her hands. "He is not in a condition to eat. Otherwise, I would have taken you to him and you would have fed him with your own hands, not mine."

Shalini and Captain Sahiram stayed almost all day around Sunil, hardly sleeping. Sahiram, broken within himself, tried to appear strong in front of Shalini. Shalini took care of Sunil along the nurse and Sahiram ji, trying to be strong in front of everyone. She has to take care of herself also as she was having 6 months of pregnancy.

Shalini came out through the fire exit and started to descend the stairs. She suddenly stopped at one stair. She gave up this time. Enough of holding back, enough of consolations, she couldn't bear anymore. Tears welled up in her eyes and she let them fall. She leaned her head against the wall and her body shook. The fluorescent light glowed brightly in the landing behind her. Suddenly she saw a shadow on the lower wall where the staircase ended. Someone was behind her. She turned around quickly wiping her tears. Sahiram stood behind her and watched her shaking body. To make sure Shalini did not feel uncomfortable, he pretended he knew nothing. If she couldn't shed those tears that she held back for so many days in front of him, then he was sure she wasn't comfortable showing her vulnerability. And he respected that.

"Everything will be all right, my child," he spoke now.

"I have a little headache, that's all, Baba," Shalini said, realizing Sahiram's presence.

Suddenly Shalini remembered something. "Baba, Dr. Nakul Sinha, Sunil's senior was asking me about you and said that he would like to meet you if he had the chance. He might want to say something to you personally."

"Don't you worry. I will meet with Dr. Nakul before I leave."

"Okay, Baba." Shalini smiled and went down the stairs heading back to Sunil's ward where he was admitted and Sahiram ji started walking to see Dr Nakul in his chamber.

The nurse came running to Dr. Lallan. Dr. Sunil had pulled the tube and now he is hypoxic (O2 saturation is low). Dr. Lallan and Dr. Shalini ran towards the bed of Sunil, where he was restless and fighting to survive. His heart rate was 140/min. and respiratory rate 40/min. Dr. Lallan intubed Sunil without wasting a second. Shalini fell on the floor. The nurse took her to the bed. Dr. Sinha and Captain Sahiram also reached there. Dr. Lallan briefed the events to Dr. Sinha and assured that now everything is alright.

"You must thank your God. He has listened to your prayers. Sunil is fighting back. It's a good sign of recovery. But his memory loss might be an issue in the days to come. But he will definitely overcome it with the time he gets to spend with his family. You can go inside and meet him."

"Do not be worried. Everything will be alright," Sahiram put his hand on Shalini's shoulder.

This was the touch of comfort she longed for from a long time ago. As if like a magic, the hopefulness of Sahiram Ji's heart seeped into her. The door creaked and both became alert. Dr. Nakul came out.

A gleam of hope spread across everyone's face. Shalini too felt confident now.

"I knew, he had to come back to me, to his wife and his unborn child and to his whole family. He will come back no matter what," Sahiram said to Shalini as they entered.

Next Day Morning:

"Shalini…" She turned and saw Lallan standing at the entrance. He called her outside. "Shalini…Sunil is better now. But you ought to take care of yourself too. Remember you are not alone anymore. Look at yourself. What have you made out of yourself in these eight days? Huh? Go home. Wash yourself. Have something healthy, filling and wholesome to eat. I am here. Don't worry at all. After all he remembers my name also. Go home." He softly tapped on Shalini's head. Shalini smiled and took up her bag from the table.

"Just let Baba know that I will be back in an hour," she asked Lallan turning once as she walked towards the lift lobby.

"Sure, I will."

⁂

The sun blasted her skin as she stood in front of their gate searching the keys in her bag. But the burning sun did not irritate her. It was a fresh escape from the closed quarters of hospital, sick and dead men and the numbing smell of Dettol, phenyl and urine.

She turned the key in the lock. There was another door. She unlocked it too. The first glimpse of the room the moment she opened the door choked her throat. The decorations were as they had left it the night of their anniversary. She first came to the dining hall. Smell of stale food items that she had prepared herself that night for the guests filled the whole room. They were perfectly arranged on the granite slab of her modular kitchen. The decorations were unharmed in this room, but the balloons had reduced in size. Champagne which was poured out into glasses for the cake cutting ceremony had evaporated. Some fried starters and appetizers that she had already served to the guests remained half eaten on beautiful dinner sets, already started going stale. The cake remained inside the box opened from all sides only waiting to be taken out of it. The candles were already planted on it. Some that were fortunate to be lit had settled in little holes burnt on the cake in a mass of molten wax with a little black burnt thread peeping out. The others stood erect or slightly inclined. She came to the wall that read "HAPPY ANNIVERSARY". It was unharmed too, only waiting to mock her.

A sob escaped her lips through her breath. The bedroom with its signs of mad rage and restless destruction haunted her. Tables overturned on the floor, decorations destroyed and torn to bits flooded the marbled floors. She closed her eyes and pictures from that day started coming to her one after another. She didn't touch a thing and straight away went for the bathroom to take a warm refreshing shower. She had to take care of her unborn too. Then she would need to pack up their bags. She knew sooner or later Sunil will be discharged and the only fight that will be left after that was to make him recover his memory.

She changed into her bath robe and went to stand under a calming shower that also calmed her mind and settled the turmoil going in her heart.

The evening visiting hours had started when she reached the hospital. Sahiram Ji had been sitting on the bench outside Sunil's ward. She did not have the state of mind to follow the general rules of an Indian household that are observed when any younger family member meets an elder one after a while. She bent to touch Sahiram's feet but he caught her by her shoulders and reprimanded her, "You don't have to do such things now. Never forget you are carrying my son's child, my grandchild. Take care."

"Sorry, Baba," she lowered her eyes.

"It's ok. Go and meet Sunil."

Shalini entered Sunil's cabin. The moment she entered, Sunil's eyes were locked on her. She wore a sky-blue saree. She came and sat beside him on her bed. For a moment he kept looking at her and then blurted out suddenly, "Shalu."Shalini didn't expect he would remember her at this stage. But then remembered his promise to her that he would remember her no matter what, even if he went into comatose. He had kept his promise. Her tears got soaked into her dried lips that broke into an extended smile. Sahiram entered and called Sunil by his name.

"Shalu, what are you doing here? Baba is watching us together," spoke out a bashful Sunil.

"Don't worry, Sunil. We are married," Shalini smiled at her own practical joke.

Dr. Nakul came inside with Lallan and spoke to Shalini and Sahiram in front of Sunil.

"Captain Saab, Sunil will get discharged within a couple of days. You must take him to your village. He must take good rest. Shalini, make sure he remains in complete mental rest. No studying and reading."

He smiled at Sahiram and shook his hands. Lallan smiled too and they left. Sahiram Ji returned to Sunil's home with Shalini and they started preparing to leave for their village in a couple of days as soon as Sunil would be discharged.

FIVE

EXECUTING GOD

S halini's brightly painted nails fiddled the teacup and her eyes were focused somewhere on the infinity through the extensive window of her chamber at the 5th floor. Sam and Ajay sat before her on the opposite side of the table. While Ajay sipped the tea Sam was busy taking notes, only interrupted by phases of contemplation compelled by the unbelievable tenacity and determination of a man.

"It took almost over a month for Sunil to be able stand on his feet. And after that my elder one was born. Ma would not let me go away with a newborn. She thought both of us along with our baby needed more care. So, we stayed back for almost three months."

Sunil stood at the window for few minutes with the coffee cup in his hand. As he slowly sipped at it, he watched the silence of a city sleeping, a silence which was intensified by the once-in-a-while heavy growling and rumbling of twelve-wheeler and fourteen-wheeler goods trucks that embarked on the village roads only at the dead of the night.

Sunil looked at his watch; it was 02:17 am in the night. His eyes spontaneously shifted to Shalini. She was fast asleep with the newborn by her side. The soft iridescence from the air conditioner that maintained a 20 degree C in the room seemed like the light from the crescent moon. The summer had grown unbearable from the last week. It was worse than the last year when Shalini used to wake up in the middle of the night and bathe from head to toe at 3 am and then her long hair would take no more than ten minutes to dry. She never complained though. She had just cut off her long locks. Sunil had watched her plight and managed to buy an air conditioner last winter when there was a sale with attractive discounts. She knew they could not afford it without the discounted price at that time when they had just taken a home in the city and started to live on their own. Sunil was still studying and not a full-time medical practitioner.

Sunil sighed. He knew even a little light from his study lamp could disturb Shalini's sleep. She had to get up frequently during the night for the baby. She was already getting very little, interrupted sleep. He wanted her to sleep soundly at least for a short time. He sipped the last drop of the coffee, put it down on the table, took up his books and notes in his hands and left the room without making a sound.

As he went out of the room he fiddled with his phone and searched his contacts frantically. Finally, he found the number he was looking for. He was in constant anxiety about his rejoining to DM. He dialed the number to College babu, the peon in his DM college. The phone rang on the other side for a few seconds before it was picked up.

"Hello…"

"Hello SGPGI college…Sunil here. Do you remember?"

"Sunil dada! How are you? How can I forget you Sunil dada? How even anyone in this college can?"

"I am better now. Can you tell me when I should re-join the college?", that I will be able to sit in exit exam at time.

"Sunil dada, let me check and I will call you tomorrow morning. As far as I know I haven't seen any such notice. The exams will be conducted on time. And you're going to join back soon."

"Thank you. I am, too, waiting eagerly. See you all soon. Good night."

He put the phone aside and sat in the living room. He continued his study as drops of perspiration slowly started to dampen his shirt in dark patches. This was his regular routine from the time he returned from his village. The days would be invested into studying for his DM and the nights would go into remembering all his medical education of his whole career up to this day, all that memory that the deadly illness had taken away from him. Every night was like a struggle to bring back his lost memory because he was a tireless warrior.

⁕❧⁕

The first day of his joining back, he was accompanied by Shalini. She supported him all along till he was inside. She was not even sure that Sunil was capable of rejoining right then with quite a few post-recovery conditions. And the ones that Sunil was having were serious enough considering his requirement for daily commuting.

He had Binocular Diplopia. It gives a dual vision through both the eyes and the images captured by both the eyes do not merge and create a single image that should be perceived in the brain. To top it and make situations even worse, he was having trouble balancing himself properly. Ataxia. The deadly combo of these two conditions apparently could make any person as good as bed ridden but not Sunil. As always, he was a fighter.

Sunil went inside and looked back to wave at Shalini who waved back to him. He went ahead with confidence knowing very well what he wanted. He was finally called in to ask about his choice of duties and selection of department. He had already seen it coming and his prompt answer was "cathlab".

"Dear Sunil, I can understand your passion for working in the cathlab but considering your own situation and the conditions you are now going through. You are not able to standup; you are having ataxia. At cathlab, you have to keep standing for 8-10 hours a day. Will you be able to do that?

"Thank you, Sunil. Only this answer was expected of you." He said with an assuring smile.

***

Shalini turned her eyes from the window to her guests who sat like stone statues in front of her. Sam and Ajay were drawn so much into the story of this brave warrior that the coffee in their cups had stopped giving off fumes. It lay there in their cups, cold and unattended.

Sam had stopped taking his notes and attentively listened to Shalini.

"Hey Sam, you forgot to take notes. Mam won't possibly have time to repeat," Ajay said doubtfully.

"Sometimes you find a story that's worth a lifelong lesson. You need to tap into it at various points in your life and every time you can't possibly expect to have a notebook with you. I have heard it, I have seen it, and I have lived it through Sunil's eyes. Do you need to take notes of something you experienced to remember it later?"

"You are right, Sam. Even I won't ever forget the story of a warrior, a real man like Sunil." Ajay agreed.

Shalini smiled at both. "And now is the time for the world to get inspired by this real warrior and true hero. And I'll make sure my book does that," Sam spoke looking at Shalini.

The door creaked and an attendant left a little girl inside the cabin and went away closing the door.

"Come here, my girl. Meet them. This is Uncle Ajay and this is Uncle Sam. Uncle Sam is writing a book about your father. He is a famous writer. Greet them," Shalini pulled the girl to herself.

"Namaste uncle Ajay. Namaste uncle Sam," the little girl spoke in haste joining her little palms together.

"Come here, little girl," Sam called the child to him.

The little girl looked at her mother for confirmation. Shalini nodded. As the girl went up to Sam he took out a chocolate bar from his bag and held it out to her. The little girl again turned to her mother. She smiled and nodded again and the girl gleefully took it from his hands. Sam put a hand on her head, "You should always be proud of your father." He suddenly remembered something and turned to Shalini.

"Mam, there's one more request. I would like to meet Dr. Sunil in person to know him better and thorough. When can we meet him? If you could kindly arrange an—" Sam was stopped by Shalini in the middle of his sentence.

"He is currently out of station to attend a conference."

"But if we just—"

"Mr. Sam, I am getting late. I need to fulfill the duties of a mother also," Shalini spoke as she got up and lifted the little child up in her arms.

"Sure Mam, but whenever Dr. Sunil returns kindly let me know or Ajay."

Shalini smiled and nodded lightly.

Ajay and Sam were walking towards the lift lobby through the corridor. Suddenly Sam spotted someone and looked at Ajay. Ajay wore a blank look on his face.

"Follow me, quick!" Sam ordered Ajay in a tone that clearly showed disappointment for Ajay's indifference and curiosity for what he saw.

"Why, what happened?"

"I just saw Dr. Sunil entering lift number 2. Come fast. We need to go by the stairs."

"What? Where did you see him? But he is not supposed to be in the hospital, right?" He started to run after Sam who was already pacing few steps ahead of him.

They started to run down the stairs competing with lift number 2. Their hurried footsteps resonated in the desolate stairwell. They descended taking few steps at a time to keep up with elevator and now they were at the ground floor. Sam was waiting with bated breath in front of the elevator. The led display board read… 2 … … 1 … … 0… He arranged himself properly to introduce. The 0 changed to -1. The elevator was going to the basement.

But the stairs have ended already. They rushed to ask the guard the way to the stairway that led to the basement.

The enormous basement looked like a spooky hall with insufficient lighting and its drop-dead silence all around. He looked this way and that but could not find the doctor. He could only see variedly colored car tops as far as he looked craning his neck. Suddenly he heard a faint, garbled sound of some conversation softly echoing from behind. He started to rush but his footsteps also echoed. Ajay clasped his arm and gestured him to walk silently.

As they slowly approached the source of the sound the garbled words started getting clear. Few words came to them…

"You're getting this wrong…" "Crime reporter…you can't do that".

It seemed like some heated argument.

Sam increased his speed and reached in front of a little cabin. The door was half open. He could see Sunil standing and another man sitting on a chair before him. Sam and Ajay quickly hid behind a car and watched.

"Sir, I repeat, you are really making a big mistake. I am Shahid Khan, a crime reporter from KLB channel."

"Well, you might be a famous crime reporter of a famous channel and much more," said Sunil, throwing a cheque book on a stool in front of the other man. "Now get lost, don't show me your face again," he says as the man extends his hand to pick it up.

Sam turns back and takes a deep breath and started walking straight ahead in fury. Ajay followed behind.

"Mr. Sam, where are you going? What has happened?"

"Sorry, Ajay. I am done with this project. Go to hell, and to hell with Sunil."

"But where are you going?" Ajay follows behind. "Our doctors are the best. If I really need to write that book, I will write one of their stories, not on one of your doctors. Your system is corrupt. Your doctors are corrupt."

"But he is a very honest doctor. I enquired at reception and they told me that Dr Sunil came to hospital just now to see a patient who had a heart attack. Wait Sam, we need to—"

"Get lost!" He vanished behind a car as he shouted. Ajay looked tensed. He stopped and took out his phone to call Abhishek. They talked for about half a minute and then Ajay put the phone back in his pocket and started to run after Sam again.

He looked everywhere in the basement, came out in the open and searched in the campus parking lot where they had parked their car. But Sam was nowhere to be found. He could not find their car. He called Sam's number several times, but his phone was switched off. He gave up and retreated not knowing what else to do.

The car drew up near the enormous multi storied office. The brightly glowing huge display read 'KLB NEWS'. Sam got off the car and walked up straight to the entrance. A guard barred his way.

"I am Sam, a writer from England. I have come to meet crime reporter Mr. Shahid Khan."

"You have to wait here. I will come and let you know."

The guard went inside as Sam waited impatiently. He went up and down the stone pathway in front of the entrance. But before long the guard appeared, "Sorry Sir, Mr. Shahid Khan is busy with an important story that needs to be readied by tomorrow morning. He gave this note and asked me to give it to you." Sam extended his hand to take the small note.

'I apologize for not being able to meet you despite being a reporter who should, by his duty, be available to all seeking him. But there's a story that needs to be completed by tomorrow morning. I am working overnight. I again apologize for not being able to spare my time for such a celebrated figure like you Mr. Sam. Hope we'll meet soon.'

Sam folded the note and called the guard back.

"What has happened again? He already said he can't meet you today. Come tomorrow."

"Kindly do me a favor. Just go once and tell him it is urgent and I need to talk to him regarding Dr. Sunil."

The guard went inside and Sam waited patiently since he knew what the answer would be.

"Mr. Sam," the guard called, "Mr. Khan has requested you to visit him right now."

⁂

Sam met Shahid outside his cabin as they exchanged formalities. Shahid then took Sam inside his cabin.

"I am a writer. I was planning my next book about a doctor's life that would inspire millions around the world and Dr. Sunil was perfect up until I saw you talk to him."

"What did you hear?"

"I saw him offer you money. Bullshit. How could I be so naïve to have come under the sway of these corrupt doctors who can turn a living man into a dead one in a moment or whenever they feel the need."

"I can understand you, Mr. Sam. It happens sometimes," Shahid said empathetically heaving a sigh.

"I was doing a crime. I was making him a hero in the eyes of the millions who read the books of writer Sam and put all their trust in whatever he writes. I was making a fool out of myself and my fans."

"Do not worry, Mr. Sam. Just wait and watch," Shahid slipped a card out of his card holder and held it out to Sam, "I am just a call away."

"Thank you so much, Mr. Khan."

"No, no. Don't thank me. I am just doing my responsibility for which I get paid enormous amounts by the end of the month."

Sam took the card and put it in his pocket.

⁂

An array of beds lay side by side, arranged perpendicularly along both the walls in the large hall. A grim smell of phenyl, urine and Dettol filled the air inside it.

A man among the patients tried to sit up on his bed with much effort but failed. He then called out another for help. "Gopal, help me get up, chhote."A man was standing near the window above his bed facing outside. Hearing his brother call him he went up to him reluctantly and pulled him up.

"*Dheere chhote*, be gentle, it hurts. Oh, see there, sister has come."

Gopal turned back tensed.

"What are you doing? Be gentle. He has just undergone a major operation," the nurse reprimanded.

"Sorry, sister. What about my card?"

"Please consult at reception counter."

Gopal walked towards the reception. People love to harass others who are in need. They are making me go round and round from pillar to post to get a single information, he thought.

"Yes please, how can I help you?" asked the neatly and pleasantly dressed woman at the reception desk.

"Can you tell me the status of the claim approval in my brother's Bhamashah card?"

"Yes. Just wait a minute…" she checked for a while and looked up at Gopal. "Ram Kumar's Bhamashah has not been approved. Please pay the bill at the cash counter."

"How can you say that? The card is not fake, how come it is not approved? There might be some problem with your hospital."

"Hundreds of patients are getting treated here through the cashless scheme. There is not a problem with our hospital."

"Then what is the problem with *bhaiya's* card?"

"I don't know, I can't say that. All I know is that his card has not been approved. Please pay the money. The bills are pending from a long time now."

"Ok, I will talk to the doctor first."

"There…the resident doctor has arrived. You can talk to him," said the receptionist.

He walked towards the corridor and shouted.

"Doctor saab! Doctor saab!"

"Yes, what happened? Keep your voice low."

"Saab, the receptionist is saying that your patient Ram Kumar's Bhamashah has not been approved. She asked to pay all the bills pending till now. Doctor saab, we are poor farmers, where could we get that much of money? Our only dependence is on Bhamashah and in kind doctors like you. Can't you kindly adjust for just one patient?"

"See… the rules are the same for everyone. If we adjust for one patient many others would come and request for the same. It won't be possible for us to adjust for so many people then. Can you understand the implications? Patient came with a heart attack. We did the procedure successfully and his urine output is low, so he needs dialysis."

"Ok, Doctor. Then I will take the patient to government hospital. His operation is done. I cannot afford to keep him here any longer."

"Shifting may be harmful in these conditions," said the doctor.

"He is alright, Doctor saab. He is speaking, wants to sit up. You are keeping him here for more money."

"Sister, please call my senior and ask him if I should discharge him, tell him about the whole scenario."

After a few minutes of conversation, the nurse kept the phone down, "Sir, he can be discharged on Gopal's own responsibility. He would be required to sign a declaration before he can get his patient discharged."

"Ok, give me whatever you need me to sign on," Gopal retorted.

The doctor gestured the sister to bring him the bond declaration paper.

"His heart is very weak. Think once before agreeing to sign it. At least let him stay tonight," requested the sister who used to attend to Ram Kumar and had grown a motherly affection towards the old man.

"No. I have decided. Bring me the paper or whatever it is."

The sister sighed and left. After forty-five minutes, completing all the discharge formalities, Gopal left with Ram Kumar in an ambulance at late evening.

"The fog is getting dense. It will not be possible to drive fast. God have mercy on him," the ambulance driver said to the old campus guard as he opened the gates. The guard nodded his head reluctantly and locked the gate after the ambulance drove off. A warm night's sleep was awaiting him near the fire of the dried leaves.

The horn blared, once, twice, thrice and then four times together in a row. The old guard unsteadily walked to the gate yawning and opened it. His sleepy eyes opened wide watching the driver who had spoken to him earlier that night.

"You came back too early dropping the patient, didn't you? It is only 4.30 am now," he asked.

"Na kaka, I have returned with him. Now open the door at the back, now. The patient has to be taken out. Give me a hand."

"But why have you returned with him? His attendant got him discharged and wanted to take him to the government hospital."

"Yes, but the patient's condition had deteriorated sharply mid-way, so we better thought to bring him back here instead of searching for other hospitals."

The guard stood and watched until the still Ram Kumar was taken out and carried towards the building. He then retreated off to his sleeping cove.

⁂

Gopal and the driver held the two ends of the stretcher and came in front of the emergency ward and called out in the deserted lobby. A nurse came out rubbing her eyes.

"What has happened?"

"My brother, Ram Kumar is a patient of your hospital. He just got discharged earlier tonight. But as I was taking him in the ambulance his condition deteriorated rapidly. So, I had to bring him back. Is there any doctor in the emergency section?"

"Wait here, I am calling someone." The nurse left and then came back soon with a young junior doctor. He came and checked Ram Kumar in the stretcher and looked up at Gopal.

"What has happened to him, doctor?" asked Gopal.

"How long did you wait after he started getting worse? Huh?" the doctor shouted at Gopal. "He is dead. Dead for so long now that we can do absolutely nothing. I am sorry. Where did you take him?"

"But your doctors got him discharged. How can you just wash your hands off a case of your own hospital and complete your responsibility by just saying sorry?" shouted back Gopal at the doctor.

The nurse intervened. "Wait, let me call the doctor in charge of this patient."

"Yes, do call him fast. He should know what he has done to my brother. He has killed him with wrong treatment."

"Go and tell him also that this patient has been dead for more than half an hour now." The young doctor said to the nurse as she was leaving.

After fifteen minutes the nurse came back with a document.

"Here, Gopal. It was you who insisted on taking the patient away in hurry accusing us of keeping patients for gaining more bed charges. Doctor saab told you that he his heart was weak and he still needed to remain in the hospital for a day or two more, under his supervision or at least until he became stable. But you know what you said and accused us of."

Gopal got agitated and entered a heated argument with the nurse and the doctor. As the voices rose, more and more people gathered around them. In the commotion and chaos one medical staff took out his phone and called a number.

"Mr. Khan, come with your media. Your story is ready."

<hr>

The old guard put the keys into the lock of the main entrance.

"Good morning, old man!" said the man standing outside the gates as the old guard put his keys into the keyhole.

He yawned in response. Then remembering his generosities he smiled animatedly, "Come in," holding the gates narrowly open for him.

No sooner had he opened the gates than few people suddenly barged in from nowhere. They briskly pushed the sweeper aside and forcefully dragged the gates wide open from both sides making an annoying grazing sound of metal scraping heavily against gravels.

"Wait! Stop! What are you doing?" shouted the startled old man.

The men ignored him like he didn't exist. As he kept on shouting more and more men and women stormed in through the gates wide open. The old guard gradually stopped yelling and stood there petrified watching the mob carrying rods, sticks and stones rush inside the premises.

Half an hour after the mob had entered the premises, two press cars from the KLB news channel drove inside the gates. Mr. Shahid Khan and few more men with cameras and microphones swiftly stepped out from the car, pushed through the armed mob and reached in front of the entrance of the building. Gopal was standing there with Ram Kumar's dead body lying by his side.

"Are you Gopal?" a microphone was held near his mouth and two cameras flashed behind the man holding it.

"Yes, I am Gopal."

The man turned back to face the camera. "This is crime reporter Shahid Khan from KLB news reporting live from a private hospital with cameramen Tapas Agrawal and Seema Seth. Right now, we are speaking to the deceased's younger brother, Gopal. Let's see what he has to say." He turned to Gopal again. "Tell us, Gopal…"

Gopal faced the camera and spoke to the media, "The doctor in charge has refused to take any responsibility. I want to speak to the senior doctor. Call him. They have killed my brother," and he started to wail loudly beating his chest.

⁂

"Do not go Sunil, I beg you, please do not go. The staff will handle this." Shalini was standing outside the cathlab door as Sunil emerged from within it after completing an emergency procedure. But Sunil was adamant. He wanted to see what has happened.

He peered down through a broken window. Almost around fifty men and women had assembled below, in front of the entrance gate. They were enraged and shouted, yelled, threw stones and bricks at the hospital building, smashed anything and everything belonging to the hospital that came in their hands. His head reeled and face turned red. But the thing that troubled and traumatized him the most were the jeers and taunts, catcalls and bad-mouthed words calling him names. He could not tolerate it any longer. Drops of perspiration flowed down his forehead and he felt the numbness in his feet return today, years after the biggest trauma in his life.

Someone from the crowd accidentally looked up and spotted him. He became startled as the man alerted the crowd. Many people started to look up one by one. Within moments the agitation in the crowd was in frenzy as they had spotted their target. He could not move as he was overwhelmed with the sprays of stones and metals that started to come up his way. A stone hit him hard in the head and he stumbled. The staff came rushing and steadied him. Blood had tainted his white coat.

They took him inside his cabin and seated him on a table. He hung his head closing his eyes for a few moments of absolute silence as his team waited with bated breath for a word to escape his mouth, ready to carry out any command. His finally raised his head.

"Leave this room for the time being," he said calmly.

"But Sir…they are—"

"I command. Leave me alone for some time. Please…" he followed his command with a request as he knew his men loved and respected him.

They started to leave the room one by one looking back every time they reached the door to check if their Sir was alright.

Everyone was gone. The shouts and yells had increased by leaps and bounds. Few more stones and varied objects flew in through the windows breaking some more glass panes as a result. The man arose from the table and walked up calmly to the door. He closed it and returned to the table.

He picked up a scalpel from the table and held it up to his eyes. The jeers and catcalls no longer seemed to disturb him. His feet ceased to feel numb.

He closed his eyes and something appeared in front of his eyes, something very familiar and very close to his heart. The sun was setting behind a short arid hill, three children stood at a distance facing it, and then they start running towards it. They run and run…up onto the hill and back down as if there were no dearth of the 'Bhodan ka pahad' challenge. If he could win every challenge in his life by keeping in mind how he won the Bhodan ka pahad race, then why not today? His mind was made up.

⁂

"Tell me, Gopal. Don't you have your Bhamashah card that pays the medical bills for poor people?" Shahid Khan asked Gopal.

"I gave them my Bhamashah, but they did not accept it. They asked me to pay the bills at the cash or else leave the hospital with the patient."

Suddenly another wave of commotion hit the crowd. Shahid khan peered behind Gopal. Dr. Sunil was walking down the final few steps inside. There were more shouts, yells and agitation in the crowd.

"This man is lying," Sunil spoke to the media. He told all the truth in front of the camera and held the document Gopal signed to the reporter.

"This signed paper cannot be a proof that Gopal killed his own brother for money," a few people from the crowd came to hit Sunil.

"Come. Hit me. Why did you stop? You are turning on people and institutes that save you and bring you back from death. Doctors are called Gods, and that is for a reason. When someone in your family goes ill, whom

154

do you rush to visit? And suddenly that God becomes a demon to you?" demanded Sunil.

"Please stop, Dr. Sunil. We have heard many such lectures before. But you cannot hide a crime with lectures. There are many such corrupt doctors in India like you, to whom money is the ultimate thing. You are a shame to this noble profession that primarily aims to save lives and not save money in back accounts. Call the police and send him behind the bars," ordered Shahid Khan.

⁂

Hand cuffs were being put on the hands that were meant to save lives holding the stethoscope and scalpels. All the time Sunil kept on muttering under his breath, "I know, I didn't do anything…"

The police dragged the respected doctor towards their car through the campus in front of everyone. Suddenly another car drove into the paved way and blocked the entrance. Out came Sam. As Shahid smiled at Sam he started speaking to the police, "Wait, inspector. This noble man is innocent. This is a trap."

"A trap? What proof do you have?" Shahid asked agitatedly.

"Wait, Mr. Khan. I will show everyone everything."

"Here is the proof," Abhishek came out of the same car with a laptop in his hand. They played a video to the inspector. The Inspector watched it intently.

Sam and Shahid are sitting inside a bar. Shahid is high after gulping multiple pegs of alcohol.

"So tell me, Shahid. How did you get to meet Dr. Sunil?"

"Ohh. He is a famous doctor. His hospital is famous. I went to meet him to ask for an advertisement from him in our paper. He blatantly refused me. He refused *me*! The famous crime reporter Shahid Khan! He is too proud of his stature and success. But what he doesn't know is that it won't take a minute for this Shahid Khan to take him down from his throne to the dusts."

"What do you mean?" Sam asks.

"Just wait till late tonight. One of his patients is going to die tonight. His death is just a phone call away. And then watch what happens to the arrogant Dr. Sunil."

"But you'll kill a person to frame him?"

"Killing of such insignificant, old people for greater purposes doesn't make a difference…"

The inspector shut the screen of the laptop and turned to Gopal. "Tell me, Gopal. Could you throw some more light on this? The video is still not completed and I don't want to watch it anymore. I want to know the rest from you."

Gopal started to tremble. "I do not know anything, saab. Please let me go."

"Tell me!" the inspector shouted on his face.

"He met me at a tea stall nearby the hospital yesterday." Gopal began, "I was very upset that the insurance company was not accepting my card and I had to deposit money of a huge amount to pay for my brother's treatment. But we are poor people saab, where would we get so much money? Our only hope is the Bhamashah, so I wanted to take my brother away without depositing money. That's when Shahid sir came and spoke to me. He assured me that I could earn money to pay for my brother's treatment at any hospital I wished to admit him, if I follow his instructions.

"As instructed, I denied paying further, created havoc and arguments at hospital and demanded discharge. But after discharge when I called him, he didn't respond. I roamed around the city in an ambulance awaiting his instructions. My brother stopped responding after some time and then Shahid sir told me to take him back to the hospital and create a scene here.

I just did what I have been asked to do by him. I lost my brother in all this drama. I am innocent, please forgive me." Gopal sobbed.

The inspector ordered his men to free Sunil and arrest Shahid and Gopal. After the crowd left, Sunil came and hugged his old friend Abhishek.

"Meet Mr. Sam. He has come a long way from London to write a book on your life, Sunil bhai. If Sam here had not called me in time, you would have been in great trouble." Abhishek laughed aloud and both Sam and Sunil joined him.

Sam shook hands with Sunil and he was elated to meet the protagonist of his book. They all got into the car along with Shalini and Ajay and left for Sunil's home.

"Dr. Sunil, tell me one thing. I just want to ask it out of curiosity. Why did you offer money to Shahid?" Sam asked.

"What our eyes see is not always the whole truth. Shahid came to my hospital asking for an advertisement in their paper. I refused. But he started threatening me saying that he was a celebrated crime reporter and he could ruin my career and everything I built in a moment and that the Lalwani hospital was closed last month because of his influence. He challenged me. So, I threw the cheque at him. The moment he reached out his hand to take it up I quickly removed it and said that I am neither going to give any advertisement nor bribe him in the fear that he might ruin my career."

"Sorry, Sunil. I am extremely sorry. I made a mistake in recognizing my protagonist, the hero of my book."

"It's ok, Sam. Sometimes our eyes betray our senses."

"But thank God, he called me. I was the one who gave him the idea of meeting Shahid in the bar." Abhishek laughed again.

"Really Abhishek, you haven't changed at all. Still beating your own drums..." and everybody broke into laughter.

The sun had just risen and the sky wore the look of a blushing bride. Two cars sped on, one showed the way and the other followed.

EPILOGUE

The sprawling bookstore was teeming with people. A long queue had formed inside the store. In the queue, a girl stood holding her little brother's hand.

"Didi… Why are we still standing here?"

"Wait bhai. I need to take a signature on the book."

"Whose signature?"

"Sshhh…We are next. I will tell you later."

"What's your name?" asked the man sitting at the table.

"My name is Anwesha. But I am gifting this book to my brother. He wants to be a doctor when he grows up."

"Very good, child. Then tell me your brother's name."

"Ashish," the girl said smiling down at her brother.

As the man signed the book and held it out to the boy. He took it and opened the title page. It read…

A MAN WITH THE WHITE COAT

With lots of love & best wishes

Dr. Sunil

www.ingramcontent.com/pod-product-compliance
Lightning Source LLC
Chambersburg PA
CBHW051438130726

47987CB00005B/2103